FINDING YOUR ANSWERS WITHIN

A 61-year-old woman from Baton Rouge, LA, shares her story: "Most of my adult life I've suffered with something happening to my throat. For no apparent reason, I would begin to choke. My throat would itch horribly until tears ran down my face. This choking would only affect one side of my throat at a time.

"I was convinced from the severity of the choking that had both sides been affected at once I would not be able to breathe. After several painful minutes the episode would end until the next time. I found no help from the medical society.

"Easter, 1986, I attended your psychic seminar in Sedona, Arizona. In the group 'back to the cause' regression I vividly experienced being a handsome youth in Missouri in 1889. When you directed us to the death experience I relived being falsely accused of some sexual behavior by a jealous woman. Without judge or jury, I was sentenced to stand behind a wagon, a rope knotted around my neck. When the horses were whipped forward, I was strangled to death.

"In the regression I imagined my throat closing, and I began to cry. Then I heard a clear message: 'You can now release this!' I did and the choking stopped and has not returned for over two years."

Books by Dick Sutphen

Finding Your Answers Within
Past Lives, Future Loves
Predestined Love
Unseen Influences
You Were Born Again to Be Together

Published by POCKET BOOKS

FINDING
YOUR
ANSWERS
WITHIN

DICK SUTPHEN

POCKET BOOKS

New York   London   Toronto   Sydney   Tokyo

An *Original* Publication of POCKET BOOKS

POCKET BOOKS, a division of Simon & Schuster Inc.
1230 Avenue of the Americas, New York, NY 10020

ISBN: 0-671-66816-1

First Pocket Books printing February 1989

10 9 8 7 6 5 4 3 2 1

POCKET and colophon are trademarks of
Simon & Schuster Inc.

Printed in the U.S.A.

*To Hunter and Cheyenne
and the New Age they will inherit*

Contents

SECTION I

METAPHYSICAL AWARENESS & TECHNIQUES

Section II

HUMAN POTENTIAL AWARENESS & TECHNIQUES

Section III

ALTERED STATES OF CONSCIOUSNESS

SECTION

I

Metaphysical Awareness & Techniques

Metaphysics is a philosophy/science of self in relationship to the universe. As a philosophy it accepts that all things are part of a central source of intelligence and energy. Everything has an independent function and yet is dependent upon all other things, with each contributing to the source. As a science it offers awareness and techniques you can use to create your own reality.

CHAPTER

1

The New Age

"I spent two years in group therapy in an attempt to resolve my feelings of being unloved by my mother," explained **Janis Edelberg** of St. Joseph, Michigan. "It didn't help. Then, in my mid-thirties, I began to explore metaphysical concepts and used hypnotic regression techniques to find the cause of my conflict. Was I ever shocked to experience a lifetime as an Indian woman whose son thought he was unloved. He was very angry with me. As I relived the experience, I realized that I loved him very much, but simply didn't know how to express it. My son in that life is my mother today.

"I learned from this experience that my mother does love me, and as a result, my relationship with her has been transformed. She hasn't changed, but I have. She still judges me, but now I can allow the negativity to flow right through me without affecting me."

As an afterthought, Janis added, "The regression probably explains an incident that occurred when I was a very small child. My mother had done something that made me angry, and I turned to her and said, 'When I get big and you get little, I'm going to spank you!' "

Irene Cummings of Bellflower, California, chanted affirmations to create her own reality. "In 1984, I had a dead-end position as a secretary for a high-tech corporation. After reading about metaphysics, I decided to see if I could use some of the techniques to improve my job situation. So I meditated and asked the Universe to manifest a position that would allow me to work with computers.

"Six weeks later, my manager called me into his office and told me that my position was being eliminated but that they would like to try me out as a data processor. This experience showed me one of the subtle truths about affirmations—word *them* carefully, because you will get just what you ask for. I began working at a computer eight hours a day, but inputting numerical data was certainly not the exciting job I'd hoped for.

"Now I began doing affirmations asking that my new job would lead me to a higher-paying, more challenging position. Three weeks later, I was temporarily 'loaned' for a week to another group in the company that needed extra help. This group worked closely with the engineering department to insure that the company's computer software functioned properly and that the technical documentation was easy to understand. I loved the work and hit it off immediately with my coworkers. The supervisor offered me a job and said he would send me to the company-run computer school to learn programming.

"Everything was perfect . . . except for my original manager. On Friday afternoon, I asked him to okay a transfer. He said it was very doubtful, but told me he'd give me a final answer Monday.

"I meditated the entire weekend, asking my Higher Self to appeal to his Higher Self. When I walked into the office on Monday, my manager told me he didn't know why but he had changed his mind. Not only could I take the new job, but he told me I would get a raise to match my new duties. I was overjoyed, and I concluded the whole process with an affirmation thanking the Universal Power and my Higher Self.

"That was three years, one big promotion, and two large raises ago. I still use New Age techniques on the job to attract the right person when I need help or to attain the best equipment. In fact, every day is a new opportunity for me to improve myself, my working conditions, and the planet."

Mari Jow of Corte Madera, California, used psychic techniques to heal herself. "My doctor discovered a dermoid cyst on my right ovary—five centimeters by five centimeters. I was very upset, because an ovarian cyst had burst eight years before and I had hemorrhaged without knowing it.

"My doctor pressed for a surgery date, saying he didn't want to wait more than a month. Nevertheless, I started visualizing healing light around the ovary during meditation and I put two written affirmations over my bed: *My cyst is shrinking every minute* and *I am healed*. I also started listening to a self-healing hypnosis tape at night. Five days later I went for another examination. The cyst was larger and my doctor insisted that it was not the kind that would go away. So I set a date for surgery later that week.

"While meditating the day after the examination, I suddenly felt a rush of energy spiraling down through my head. It was as though every cell in my body was jiggling around at an accelerated speed.

"Upon entering the hospital later that week, I urged my gynecologist to do an exploratory before removing the cyst. He was reluctant. 'It will add at least an hour to the time you're under anesthesia,' he said, 'and it's a waste of time because the cyst must come out.' I urged him to do it anyway. When I awoke in the recovery room my gynecologist was telling me how lucky I was. 'I've never seen anything like it!' he exclaimed. 'I did the exploratory and was amazed to find the cyst was gone—completely!' "

Janis, Irene, and Mari are typical of the growing number of people who are using commonly accepted metaphysical techniques to find their answers within —New Agers who have embraced a larger reality.

During 1987 and 1988, I conducted New Age seminars in fifty cities. Accompanied by my family and a team of five, we traveled from one coast to the other and back again in a Silver Eagle—a specially designed bus used by many entertainers because of its fantastic comfort and smooth-as-silk ride. While we were planning the tour, I told my California staff, "I want to go to Omaha, Nebraska, and other midwestern cities."

They responded with a combined, "What? Of the 150,000 people on our mailing list, only two hundred are in the entire state of Nebraska. There's no interest in the New Age there."

"I believe there's a market," I insisted. "Traveling on the Eagle, we can do seminars in towns where it's just not economically feasible to fly in with a whole team. We're also going to Colorado Springs, Colorado."

"Colorado Springs?" they moaned. "That's a military town—one of the most conservative in the West! You're crazy, Richard!"

As it turned out, even with a minimum of publicity there were over four hundred people at the seminar in Colorado Springs and 372 attended in Omaha. This was typical of our reception everywhere.

During each seminar, I explained, "As we've traveled across the country, I've done a lot of radio and television interview shows. The first question every host seems to ask is, 'What's the difference between the New Age and the current age?' Here's how I respond: New Agers look for their answers within. The rest of mankind seeks answers outside themselves. The established religions provide their followers with answers in the form of dogma. New Agers find their own answers by using techniques for inner exploration. The medical profession treats the disease with drugs and surgery, but New Agers tend to take responsibility for their own illnesses and seek natural, holistic methods for healing the person as well as the symptoms. Society points its collective finger and blames others for what is, but New Agers believe that they have created their present incarnation and karma. Governments thrive on conflict and defense budgets, but New Agers embrace the unity of humankind. New Age awareness seems to be evolving naturally within the hearts of a segment of humanity, and millions are responding to an inner calling. Obviously you're one of them or you wouldn't be here."

Jeremy P. Tarcher offers another explanation of the New Age movement. *(Tarcher is president of Jeremy P. Tarcher Inc., a Los Angeles publishing house, and this condensed version of his editorial, "New Age As Perennial Philosophy," first appeared in a* <u>Los Angeles Times</u> *Book Review Endpapers in February 1988.) He says:*

No one speaks for the entire New Age community. Within the movement, there is no unanimity as to how to define it or even that it is sufficiently cohesive to be called a movement. However, I believe that the following statements would satisfy a very large portion of the people who associate themselves with it.

First of all, don't think of the words *New Age* as representing a specific period of time. It is not the

Ice Age, or the Renaissance. Rather, it is a metaphor for a process of striving for personal growth through which millions of people are trying to become more fully awake to their inherent capacities.

Like every other movement, whether religious, political, economic, or philosophical, the New Age is ultimately based upon a group of assumptions about the place of humanity in the cosmos. At the heart of New Age thought is the idea that humans have many levels of consciousness and that, with the exception of a limited number of spiritual geniuses throughout history, we essentially live in a walking sleep that keeps us from a balanced, harmonious, and direct relationship with God (however you understand that concept), nature, each other, and ourselves.

Broadly stated, this world view is that: (1) The everyday world and our personal consciousness is a manifestation of a larger, divine reality; (2) humans have a suppressed, or hidden, Higher Self that reflects, or is connected to the divine element of the universe; (3) this Higher Self can be awakened and take a central part in the everyday life of the individual; and (4) this awakening is the purpose or goal of human life. This set of ideas, which Aldous Huxley called 'the Perennial Philosophy,' is perhaps the oldest underlying spiritual perspective of humanity and is inherent, though often buried, in the practice of traditional religion. In this sense, the New Age is not new—it is ancient.

Most, but definitely not all, people who consider themselves in the movement feel that they have had some kind of awakening experience that changed their views of the world and of their goals in life. It has, in consequence, changed the way they live and communicate about their lives. Although it is often difficult to do so and makes them stand out in embarrassing ways, New Agers try to act upon this perspective because it seems to contain a deeper meaning than the experiences of their previously 'unawakened' selves.

The process of awakening is most commonly called self-realization, enlightenment, or transformation. The transformation process is confusing, partial, and uneven. The person striving for 'enlightenment' does not quickly or permanently embody what these words imply, as the vision of what one might become if one were to be 'enlightened' is invariably larger than the ability of the individual to contain or reflect it.

Inevitably, this preliminary self-realization, this connection to new ideas and higher values, is accompanied by a massive shaking up of the individual's traditional perspectives. These are often replaced by more open, experimental, idiosyncratic ideas and behaviors.

Who are the people who adopt New Age ideas? The press would have you believe they're crackpots because it makes better headlines. But assigning the typical journalist a story on the New Age is like sending a reporter who knows nothing about baseball to cover the World Series. In reality, New Agers are ordinary people who have expanded their awareness and embraced a new way of thinking.

One Friday morning, while I was writing this chapter, a friend called from London. She is married to a well-known film director and they were out of the country on location. Part of the conversation went like this:

"What else are you working on besides the new book?" I asked.

"We're thinking about working on having another child," she answered with a laugh. "But my Higher Self told me it would be another girl. I want one girl and one boy. So I asked, 'Why can't I just have a boy?' I was told, 'If you have a boy you won't have any more. I'd like you to have five children, but since that isn't possible, if you have another girl next, you'll be willing to try a third time for a boy.'"

A weird conversation? Not to me. Not to her. For years, she has successfully sought the guidance of her Higher Self and the advice has always proved accurate and helpful.

After that phone call, I decided to observe how many times I saw New Age techniques used in the next forty-eight hours. That afternoon another friend, a country singer, called my wife, Tara, to talk over two recording production offers. The singer is a student of A Course in Miracles and had been meditating on the two possible choices. Tara added her own practical advice, combined with some Higher Self attunement, and a decision was made.

That evening, we watched a videotape of a tennis match that had been broadcast earlier in the day. "I just saw who's going to win," Tara announced with a smile.

"Don't tell me the name. Just write it down and we'll see," I suggested, although I knew she'd be right. Even when a game is broadcast live, she can close her eyes and accurately visualize who will be listed as the winner at the end of the match. She is always correct when there is no pressure and nothing is at stake, and this time, too, she was right.

Early Saturday morning, I played tennis at our club with my brother-in-law, Jason McKean, and my son, William, who is twelve. Skipping the necessary stretching, I went right into a warm-up volley and then the game. Ten minutes later I tore one of my calf muscles and spent the rest of the match hobbling painfully around the court. Already suffering the pangs of "tennis elbow," I now had what is romantically called "tennis leg."

My mother-in-law, Marianne McKean, was visiting from Alaska. She's a registered nurse, and she immediately sat me down and began to meditate, concentrating blue healing light through her hands and generating an intense heat. We then iced the leg and by the next morning I was walking normally—no aches, no pains—as if nothing had ever happened.

That evening, we talked about other ways we had used metaphysical and New Age techniques during the past forty-eight hours. "It's so hard to separate them from anything else we do, they're so much a part of us," Tara said. Everyone agreed. Then she added, "Every day I visualize Lacy [our collie who is in ill health] on a bed of amethyst crystals and send her healing."

"I chant every morning as I drive to work," Marianne said. "This draws in spiritual energy and then I send it out to everyone in the family, visualizing each person individually."

The conversation quickly turned to recent, more dramatic events. A few weeks before, Tara had been in the hospital to deliver our daughter, Cheyenne, by Caesarian section. The day after the birth, an infection developed and Tara was put on antibiotics, but she didn't want to take them because she was breastfeeding. She was still running a high fever during evening visiting hours when well-known metaphysical author Jess Stearn and two other friends came to see her. I suggested we join forces and do a healing. The four of us laid our hands over Tara's abdomen while each one, silently and in his own way, drew down and released the healing energy. A nurse appeared during the process, thermometer in hand, and looked at us as though we were crazy, but she allowed us to finish before taking Tara's temperature. Then, frowning, she shook the thermometer down again and took Tara's temperature a second time. The results: 98.6 degrees, a normal reading.

As a registered nurse, Marianne can administer anesthesia. She described in detail how she channels Universal Energy to the dentist and his patients, and how her spirit guides actively support her work. "Doctor K. tells me, 'I do the same procedures day in and day out, but when you're not here, nothing ever goes as well,'" Marianne said, beaming.

"Does he know you use metaphysical techniques?" I asked.

"Oh, no," she replied. "He's a born-again Christian!"

I laughed. "Better, then, the gentle persuasion of example than the rhetoric of ideology."

"Your stock market story is a perfect example of combining the esoteric with the real world," Tara said.

As trustee I am responsible for investing the money in our corporate pension fund, and after some discouraging experiences with commission stock brokers, I began to study the market and make some investment decisions on my own. After reading a lot of books, talking with a friend who was a professional financial adviser, and subscribing to several extensive newsletters, I did quite well with our money during the first year I managed it myself. During August 1987, I carefully planned over a hundred thousand dollars worth of pension fund investments—seven funds with the best profit projections for the next year—all conservative, with long "all-weather" track records in low-risk categories.

I finished my final calculations late one night and planned to visit our discount broker in West Los

Angeles the following morning. But as I got up to leave my studio and go to bed, I felt very uneasy. "This is ridiculous. I know my calculations are correct and my decisions fit our needs," I told myself as I climbed into bed. But the uneasiness persisted and I simply could not drop off to sleep.

After lying there a while I sighed and got up, returned to my studio, and sat at my desk. Taking out my crystal pendulum, I held it between my hands and visualized an intense white light coming down from above and entering the crown chakra. Softly, I recited my ritual. "I call out to the positive powers of the Universe, to my tribe and those who share my energy. I seek Thy protection from all things seen and unseen, all forces and all elements. In Thy Divine Name, I open to the light. I offer my body, my mind, and my spirit to the light. Let Thy Divine Will and mine be as one. I seek to expand the light within and I seek a tranquil mind and harmony with the Divine Law. I thank Thee in advance for the unfolding visions, spiritual awareness, and healing that awaits me. As it is above, so it is below. I ask these things in Thy Name. I beseech it and I mark it. And so it is."

Opening my eyes, I laid the chain over my index finger, braced my arm on the desk, and allowed the quartz crystal to swing freely. "Should I invest the pension fund money in the stock funds I've chosen?" I asked aloud. The crystal swung violently counter-clockwise, the direction I had programmed to mean "No!"

"Have I chosen the wrong stocks?" Again, the crystal responded with the "no" pattern.

"Should I invest in any stocks?" Yet again the answer was a clear-cut, unequivocal "no."

"Should I put the money in Certificates of Deposit?" Instantly the crystal began to swing clockwise, a resounding "Yes!"

The following morning I said to Tara, "I've got to go into L.A. to buy the pension fund stocks, but I'd feel better if you'd use your techniques to see if I've made the right choices." I handed her a computer print-out showing the investments I'd picked.

"Sure," she responded and sat down in the living room with her Tarot cards. Half an hour later she came back out to my studio. "I don't like it at all," she said. "I've worked with the cards and the I Ching, and everything is negative."

"Negative?" I queried.

She bit her lip, afraid that she had hurt my feelings. "Really negative, Richard," she said apologetically. "I wouldn't invest the money in those stocks or in anything else right now."

Six weeks later, on "Bloody Monday," October 19, 1987, the Dow fell 508 points.

Can I count on that kind of support next time? I don't think it's guaranteed, but I'll certainly use my own methods to check out future investment decisions before I act. It's true that at times I've focused all my energy on healings and nothing *has* happened. But to me it's more important that sometimes, something has happened. There is certainly no sure-fire New Age formula because there are always many internal and external variables—karmic variables are probably also a factor—yet obviously, we're on the threshold of a great new awareness. Searching for answers is what makes the adventure fun. I see New Agers as modern pioneers, only this time the territory waiting to be discovered is our own inner potential.

CHAPTER

2

Learning to Receive Your Answers Within

It is easier to find your answers within if you're in an altered state of consciousness. It can be a light, eyes-open altered state, or a deep, eyes-closed level. You can call it self-hypnosis, meditation, or any other name, but they all refer to the same effect: reducing the cycle-per-second activity of your brain from the beta level to the alpha level. When you're in alpha, you are in an altered state of consciousness. And the deeper you are into alpha, the deeper the altered state.

This isn't very mystical. Research has shown that two-thirds of the time you spend watching television you are in an alpha level—an eyes-open trance. When you go to bed and begin to relax, the cycle-per-second activity of your brain slows from beta to alpha, then to theta and finally to delta, which is deep sleep.

This doesn't mean that you "trance out" and lose awareness of what happens in an altered state. Your conscious mind remains involved, but as you relax into the alpha range your attention span narrows to focus on just one thing, and the filters that normally

block access to subconscious memories and superconscious awareness are temporarily removed. Once
you learn to *receive* and *trust* in alpha, the adventure
really begins.

The last chapter of this book offers my altered-state-
of-consciousness technique, plus instructions on how
to work safely by yourself or with another person and
how to make your own tapes. I will refer to this as *the
technique* in other chapters.

Learning to receive your answers within really
begins with understanding our reason for being here
on earth at this time. First, we all have our individual
karma to resolve and dharma to fulfill. Karma is the
Law of Cause and Effect. Classically, it is best expressed, "As you sow, so shall you reap." The effect of
positive or negative deeds is balanced over a sequen-
tial series of lifetimes, resulting in perfect justice.
Dharma is your duty to yourself and to society.
Karma conditions you, through your experiences, to
create the character required to fulfill your dharma.

Second, we all share the same ultimate purpose to
learn to let go of fear and to express unconditional
love. To resolve our karma, we must let go of all the
fear-based emotions: anger, selfishness, jealousy, hate,
greed, possessiveness, guilt, envy, anxiety, insecurity,
inhibitions, egotism, malice, blame, resentment, repression. It is these fears that keep us earthbound,
returning lifetime after lifetime.

As we let go of fear, we naturally raise our vibrational rate, which is sometimes called our level of awareness. We are all born with a vibrational rate we earned
in the past as the natural result of how we lived our
previous lives. How you have lived your life from your
birth up until this moment dictates your current
vibrational rate. If you have lived your life expressing
excessive fear-based emotions, you have probably
lowered your vibrational rate. But the other side of

fear is love. To raise your rate, you must learn to express unconditional love, which is the acceptance of others without judgment, without blame, without expectation. As we rise above our fears, we open to express unconditional love naturally; the more we express unconditional love, the easier it becomes to let go of fear.

All too often, however, we forget to apply the non-judgmental attitude of unconditional love to ourselves. We all have two selves: an ego-self, which is constantly thinking and judging, and a natural-self, which is quiet and accepting. Harmony can exist between these two selves only when your mind is quiet—only then can you attain peak performance levels in whatever you do, whether it is your work, your leisure activities, or your psychic awareness. You perform your best not when you are *trying,* but when you respond naturally.

In Zen, this is called "muga," which means an attitude of action in which you do not feel that "I am doing it." You cease to calculate or dwell on winning or losing. You simply do your best, responding to an inner direction that carries you effortlessly through the experience.

For years, I've told the audiences in my seminars "Everyone is psychic, and we all have the ability to become fairly good psychics. It's like developing any skill. Let's assume we were all to take tennis lessons this afternoon. Once you understand the basics, if you're willing to practice regularly, you will soon become a fair tennis player. Some of you may have natural hand-eye coordination, so you might quickly become excellent players. But with regular practice, everyone can play the game on some level. The same is true of psychic development. Some of you have more natural ability than others, and once you understand how to receive this kind of awareness and are willing to practice regularly, you will become excellent psychics. Regardless of innate capacities, though, everyone in the room can develop a certain level of psychic skills."

As often as I've used tennis as an analogy for expanding psychic perception, though, it wasn't until I became personally addicted to the game that I discovered the truth of the analogy. As two individuals obsessed with learning to be better players, Tara and I soon learned that we played our best when we were not thinking how, when, or where to hit the ball, but just let it happen.

Non-judgment of self and others doesn't mean ignoring faults or mistakes. It means observing "what is" without labeling it bad or good. Labeling is the ego-self getting in its own way.

In tennis, as in psychic performance, judgment leads to emotional reactions that cause you to tighten up and try too hard, thus reducing your performance level. W. Timothy Gallwey wrote a Zen view of the sport called The Inner Game of Tennis (Random House, 1974). In it, he explains that judging your game creates tightness, rather than the fluidity required to move quickly and accurately, while relaxing produces smooth strokes. Also, it's important to remember that errors are part of learning how to play. Just don't judge them as bad, but accept them as what is, and a natural, speedy correction can follow.

To illustrate, Gallwey recounts a tennis story from his days as a teaching pro. He was working with a group of five women and told them he would hit each woman six running forehands to help them in observing their footwork. He said, "Get in touch with how your feet move into position and whether there is any transfer of weight as you hit the ball." There was no right or wrong to think about—the women were just supposed to keep their attention on their feet.

When Gallwey hit the balls, he said nothing. There were no positive or negative judgments, and the women were absorbed in the simple process of observing their footwork. After thirty balls, however, he pointed out that they had hit every ball over the net. It was just an observation, but his tone of voice showed how pleased he was.

The next woman remarked, "Oh, no, you would have to say that just before my turn." Gallwey noticed that on the next thirty balls, the women were frowning, their footwork was more awkward, and eight balls went into the net. They had focused on trying to keep the balls from hitting the net—trying to live up to an expectation, a standard of right and wrong they felt had been set for them.

Gallwey saw that this is how the ego-self works. It is always looking for approval and trying to avoid disapproval. The women's ego-selves reasoned, "If he is pleased with high performance, he'll be displeased with the opposite." That little bit of approval had established a standard of "good" and "bad" in their minds, a standard they felt they had to meet in order to earn his approval. The result: reduced concentration and ego-self interference.

Whether you're playing tennis or perceiving psychic impressions, neither negative nor positive thinking works. *Non-thinking is what works!* The idea is to *concentrate* without *thinking;* to keep your mind focused on what you are doing and the results you want to achieve, without focusing on "how to do it." Don't try to *make* it happen . . . just *let* it happen.

I first began teaching psychic perception techniques and working with group hypnotic regression in 1971. In the seventeen years since, I've found there is an audience receptivity pattern that never varies by more than a few percentage points. For example, if I am preparing the group for a past-life regression, I start with an introductory talk followed by explanations and exercises on how to receive impressions. About 85 percent of them will receive well the first time they try and will continue to improve as the seminar progresses. After additional explanations and maybe a demonstration, another ten percent of the group who have been trying too hard will begin to receive vivid impressions.

The remaining five percent seem to be either incapable of self-trust or else they have unrealistic expectations. They expect to perceive their impressions in a particular way, and when their experience doesn't live up to their expectation, they refuse to accept what they do perceive. Their attitude is "I won't accept it unless it happens the way I expect it to."

Their beliefs literally block them from accepting that their experiences are meaningful. To help them attain the results they desire, I have to overcome their beliefs about subjective reception, which is also what I have to do with my readers. I have to convince you to do two things: 1) to trust yourself, and 2) to let go of your expectations. If you are willing to do these things, there is no reason you should not receive vivid impressions while in an altered state of consciousness. Psychic perception is a simple process of self-trust, but it is different for everyone and this seems to be what frustrates some people.

Let's begin with the primary misconception about opening to subjective awareness: the idea that you have to see pictures in your mind, like a movie. I've worked with over 80,000 people in seminars and have conducted hundreds of individual past-life regressions. And just because you receive subjective impressions in one way at one time doesn't necessarily mean that you'll receive impressions the same way the next time. I only go into a very light trance when hypnotized, but in all my years of exploring past-life regression I have received impressions in each of the ways I'll describe next, and on a few occasions even as vivid dreams.

Some of the best subjects I've ever worked with have claimed not to see a thing. Yet, because they have been willing to trust their thoughts or feelings, they have experienced very important regressions or Higher Self sessions. And my follow-up research has often proved their stories to be valid.

The most common way people receive subjective impressions in an altered state is as a fantasy, similar to what you might experience when remembering a situation you've been in. Think back to the last time you had a fight with someone, and how you later relived it in your mind. In retrospect, you probably saw how you could have been more clever and imagined yourself responding with the perfect comeback. You knew it was just wishful thinking, but as you mentally relived the encounter, it became quite real. Or think back to your last good sexual fantasy; you imagined it and became emotionally involved with the inner images, yet all the time you were fully aware of your surroundings and knew you were creating the fantasy.

Another way people receive subjective impressions is in the form of single pictures, scenes, or images that change or shift, like watching a slide show or looking at snapshots. Others will hear an inner voice telling them about the things they are trying to explore. Occasionally, an individual will see words and literally read them, as if scanning an unseen book.

Next, be aware that you can perceive impressions either as an observer or as a participant. For example, in past-life regression most people perceive impressions as an observer, as if watching themselves on a movie screen in their minds. But some will relive the situation as though they were looking through the eyes of their former selves, re-experiencing events that occurred in another time and place.

Sometimes you may start out experiencing a regression as an observer, but as you become more familiar with the lifetime, you'll switch viewpoints and begin to relive the events as a participant. As a participant you are more likely to become emotionally involved, although you wouldn't experience the physical pain of the former incarnation. Anytime you get emotionally upset in an altered state, you can always awaken by counting from one to five and saying "wide awake."

Some of the finest hypnotists in the country have regressed me. Extensive research has proved, time and again, the historical accuracy of my regressive experiences. *Yet, in every past-life regression I've experienced, I've felt as though I were making up the answers.* Sometimes, I'd receive vivid visual impressions; other times, only a fleeting thought would pass through my mind. But instead of questioning the origin of the thought, I trusted myself enough to verbalize it. Then, after the regression, I would do some research to see if what I'd said was valid. And almost without fail, if research could uncover the information, what I'd received was proved accurate.

Researching my parallel life as Ed Morrell meant examining the records of San Quentin and Folsom prisons, plus microfilm records of many turn-of-the-century California newspapers. There is certainly no way I could have ever been exposed to this information earlier in my life, then forgotten about it—a frequently voiced explanation by critics of hypnosis, past-life regression, and psychic phenomena. What I related in the regressions proved to be true, even to the most minute, seemingly insignificant detail. I even disproved a couple of recorded facts about Morrell's life.

As a result of my years of altered-state, past-life experiences, I've learned that I can trust my mind—even when I think I'm *making it up*. I also want to add that everyone I've ever worked closely with in regression has also initially felt they were making it up.

How light or deep an altered-state-of-consciousness subject you are has nothing to do with the accuracy of your perceptions. Anyone can easily attain an alpha level and perceive subjective impressions. The hard part is trusting yourself enough to take the impressions seriously.

Whether I'm hypnotizing a subject in person or with my prerecorded tapes, my goal is always to put the body to sleep but to keep the mind fully alert on all levels. The subject remains aware of his or her environment, but their concentration is focused on one thing and they are receptive to suggestions.

Let's do a quick preparatory exercise I use in my seminars. I maintain that we all have a resident windbag in our head. He never shuts up. I call him the Babbler because he chatters constantly about anything and everything. So what I want you to do now is to put the book down, close your eyes, and just listen to the Babbler for a few moments before you read on.

Did you hear him? When I ask this in a seminar training room in front of a group of two hundred people, there will invariably be five or six who raise their hands to indicate that they didn't hear anything. Then I explain that Babbler was the little voice that kept saying, "Voice, what voice? I don't hear any voice."

Babbler is always there in your mind, unless you are one of the very few highly trained individuals who have developed the ability to still their minds completely and totally for short periods. This is usually only accomplished through extensive meditation or

Zen training. So you are always going to hear this mental babbling as you seek awareness within. But sometimes while you're in an altered state of consciousness, what you hear may actually be valid information about your past, or awareness from your Higher Self, or channeling from your guides or Masters.

The next exercise relates to subjective visual impressions. Read my instructions, then close your eyes and visualize. We'll do it in several steps.

INDUCTION TECHNIQUE

To begin, I want you to make yourself very comfortable, close your eyes, and do some deep breathing for a couple of minutes. Yoga breathing is simply inhaling very deeply, then holding your breath as long as you comfortably can before letting it out slowly, through slightly parted lips. (Keeping your lips slightly parted while exhaling allows you to retain the moisture in your mouth so you are more comfortable.) When you think you've exhaled the breath completely, contract your stomach muscles and push the rest of it out. Then repeat the process. This form of diaphragm breathing will quickly relax you. So stop now and spend two minutes breathing deeply.

Now that you are relaxed, I'd like you to close your eyes and visualize your bathroom at home. You're very familiar with your bathroom, so picture it in vivid detail. Next, place yourself in the room. Where are you? Are you in the doorway looking in, or standing in the center of the room? Place all the main elements in the room: the toilet, tub or shower, the washbasins, the towel racks, the mirror. Look at the towel racks. What color are the towels hanging on them? Are they arranged neatly, or are they tossed over the racks? Look down at the floor. What is covering it—carpet, tile, hardwood? Look closely and notice the color and texture of your bathroom floor. Where is your toothbrush? Exactly what color are the walls? Are there any windows? Close your eyes and take five minutes to do this exercise.

You were perceiving visual impressions of your bathroom with your eyes closed. I think you will agree that "perceive" is a more accurate word than "see" for what you just experienced. Now, let's add another element. Altered-state visual impressions are enhanced when you can use your other physical senses: touch, taste, smell, and hearing. As an example, I'd like you to close your eyes once again and return to your bathroom, only this time you will perceive what it feels like to stand in your bathroom in your bare feet. You're very familiar with the sensation. The idea is to recapture it subjectively, then explore on your own. Mentally experience combing your hair in front of the mirror, showering, brushing your teeth. Take five minutes to do this now.

Remember what I said at the beginning of this chapter? Neither the ability to play tennis nor the ability to receive psychic impressions develops instantly. But the more you practice, the faster you can learn to do it well. When you mentally "remembered" your bathroom, you were dealing with the known. Now, let's explore the unknown by making up a visual impression.

Close your eyes and visualize an American Indian on horseback. You can use images from movies, pictures, and drawings you've seen, or even memories from your own past lives. Create the scene in vivid detail. First, visualize an environment for the horse and rider. It might be the plains, the desert, mountains, a forest, a lake, or a village. Attempt to capture the feel of the environment. Is it hot or cold? Night or day? What is the season of the year? Can you feel the air on your skin? What scent does the breeze carry . . . or is there a breeze? If you're in the desert, can you taste the dust? Close your eyes and determine the surroundings. Then we'll work on the horse and Indian.

Now, let's look closely at the horse. Is it large or small? What about the color—is it buckskin, bay, sorrel, roan, appaloosa, or pinto? And what about the Indian? What is he wearing on his feet—boots, shoes, moccasins, or is he barefoot? What is he wearing on his lower body—a breechcloth, buckskins, or pants? What color are they and what are they made of? What is the Indian wearing on his upper body? Any necklaces, bracelets, arm bands, or body paint? Look at his hair. Notice the color. Is it long or short? How is it worn? Is he wearing anything on his head? And I'd like you to look in his eyes. What do you see in his eyes? Take at least five minutes to complete these mental pictures in vivid detail.

Once again you have perceived impressions with your eyes closed. You remembered them or made them up, and they appeared in your mind. This is the very least you should perceive in an altered state of consciousness when you are looking for your own answers. In seminars, people have challenged me by saying, "But I'm familiar with my bathroom. I'm just pulling the impressions out of my memory." I agree with them. Of course, that's what you're doing. And the pictures from your past lives are as valid as those of your bathroom—they are your memories, too.

Your subconscious mind is a memory bank containing a record of every thought, word, and deed from this life you are currently living . . . and all of your past lives. Your superconscious mind is the 95 percent of your awareness that is not normally used. Within it lies the Higher Self and access to the "collective unconscious" of all mankind.

To move on to the next phase in this process, please skip to the last chapter and review the technique described there. Practice going in and out of an altered state of consciousness several times.

Next, go into an altered state of consciousness and ask yourself to recall and re-experience, to the best of your ability, events from your past. I'll provide a list—you can add to it or come up with your own. You can choose to remember what to ask yourself, have someone else direct the process, or make a tape of the list. The idea is to mentally capture every detail of your memories, including the emotions. Don't intellectualize the process; simply observe the very *first* impression that surfaces and flow with it for a minute or two. Some situations will carry more psychic energy than others.

1. Recall something that happened to you between the ages of one and ten.
2. Recall a situation you experienced between the ages of ten and twenty.
3. Recall something about your parents.
4. Recall a teenage encounter with the opposite sex.
5. Recall a teenage encounter with the same sex.
6. Recall a time in your past when you were rejected.
7. Recall a time when you were extremely happy.

8. Recall a positive memory of the person closest to you.
9. Recall a negative memory of the person closest to you.
10. Recall an event that occurred last week.
11. Recall a time when you were ashamed.
12. Recall a proud moment in your life.
13. Recall a time when you engaged in a form of play, whether a sport, hobby, or other recreation, alone or with others, and enjoyed it.

And now, using the awakening technique of counting up from one to five, say the words, "wide awake."

The above exercise is a good way to shake up your subconscious mind. You are bounced from one emotional extreme to another—ideal preparation for altered-state work, such as "back to the cause" regressions.

When you are working in an altered state and seeking psychic answers, it's important to realize that no little red light goes on in your head announcing a psychic revelation. I've worked with many of the top psychics in the country, and all of them receive their information the same way you do—as a thought, or as a thought combined with a feeling, or as a visual impression. The professional psychic simply trains himself to focus his attention when seeking understanding, and to listen to his thoughts. For example, he may send out a thought, such as, "What is the real problem behind Mary's constant stomach pains?" He then empties his mind and listens to his own thoughts as they come back to him: "Mary is developing an ulcer and should be examined by a doctor immediately." Or he might perceive a fantasy-like visualization in which he sees a dark spot developing in Mary's stomach, which he then interprets through his own symbol system.

Once you know how to ask, it all boils down to self-trust. You learn to trust yourself as a result of your experiences. One of the most difficult things you will have to do is trust your initial impressions as opposed to your ego-self. I've often done an ESP demonstration using colored cards to make this point. There are a total of twenty cards, four each of five different colors: red, blue, yellow, green, and black. Standing in front of the audience, I appear to shuffle the cards, but the deck is actually stacked.

Then, picking up one card at a time, I look at the colored side and telepathically send them the color. After allowing several seconds for them to perceive it, I turn the card over so they can see what I was sending. To make my point about trusting the *very first impression,* all four blue cards will appear in sequence, one after the other. The audience has seen me shuffle the cards, so they expect random colors to appear. After they have experienced three blue cards in a row, and I begin to telepathically send the color of the fourth card (also blue), the majority of the group allows their conscious mind to get in the way and intellectualize. For most of them, the first impression was blue, but then the Babbler starts in: "Well, there were three blues in a row, and he did shuffle them in the beginning, so the odds are very much against this card being blue. Let's see, it must be green, not blue. That's it. Green!"

I show the seminar participants the blue card to make my point. In seeking psychic guidance, trust the very first thought you receive, and follow it to see where it takes you.

Now that you have a basic understanding of how to prepare your consciousness to perceive psychic impressions, it's time to look at some of the primary areas we will be exploring.

CHAPTER

3

Spirit Guides

Maidie Moore Garcia, Gulfport, MS: "A few years ago, I lived in Chicago. One night, while walking the nine blocks from the church to my house, I heard footsteps behind me. They crunched lightly in the frozen snow and I thought it was another woman. As I approached an alley, an inner voice said loudly, 'Gal, cross the street.' I didn't respond immediately. 'Do it now, don't look back! Hurry, go toward the lights.' This time I followed instructions. When I got to the drugstore, I looked back to see a tall man in dark clothes with white gym shoes standing at the entrance to the alley.

"I later learned that an hour after my experience with the inner voice, a woman was pulled into that alley, robbed, raped, and beaten. The victim remembered that her attacker was a tall man wearing white gym shoes."

Elaine Grace Cipolloni, Dothan, AL: "My spirit guides play a regular part in my life. Sometimes their communications are about trivial things, but on other occasions they concern quite important matters. Here are a couple of examples:

"Halfway through a grocery shopping expedition, just about the time I reached the ice cream section, an inner voice said, 'Where are your car keys?' I couldn't imagine why my guides were asking that, since I assumed the keys were in my purse as always. Just to be certain, I looked for them, but to no avail. 'Don't buy the ice cream. It will melt. You locked your keys in the car,' they said. They were right. I called my husband, who came quickly, but he had given his set of car keys to our son. A policeman eventually used a door-opening device to open the car.

"Another incident concerns a three-month effort by my guides to get me to purchase a steering wheel cover. They kept directing me into stores, then to the displays of the covers. I couldn't imagine why they were doing this, so I ignored their efforts—I didn't want a steering wheel cover, I was quite happy with my car the way it was. Finally, one day as I was driving through a residential neighborhood near our house, they warned me not to drive any farther, to either stop or to turn off at a friend's house and call my husband to take me home. Again, I ignored the inner voices. Within two minutes, I was involved in a head-on collision. I was lucky; I only gashed my chin on the steering wheel. But even that could have been avoided if I had listened to my voices."

Randall D. Rost, APO NY: "I was working on a railroad shuttle, moving railcars from one side of the plant to the other. My job was to guide the cars down the tracks and switch tracks to place the cars in the proper areas. I was daydreaming when I heard an inner voice scream, 'Randy!' It was the unmistakable voice of my uncle who had died a year before. I looked up just in time to realize that if I had switched tracks, as I was starting to do, I'd have derailed the cars right on top of me."

* * *

While still new to self-hypnosis, I did considerable experimenting with trance depth. To go deeper you have only to relax your body from head to toes, over and over, until you can hardly feel a thing. Then count yourself down, then down again, and yet another time, further down. On one particular occasion, from the darkness behind my closed eyes, an attractive woman appeared and told me her name was "Neeta" and she was my spirit guide. She had long, jet-black hair and appeared to be in her mid-thirties. She was dressed in tan leather. During our "conversation" via "thought language" or instantaneous thought transference, she explained that we had shared a lifetime as part of a large group or tribe of people who lived by metaphysical ideals and practiced esoteric technologies.

According to Neeta, she had been with me since my birth in this lifetime and would remain with me throughout my life. While out of body on the other side, you are not idle; serving as a spirit guide is a way to work through karma and to evolve spiritually. Neeta explained that I had helped her many times in the past. By taking the job as my guide, she was repaying a debt and helping herself at the same time.

I asked her what she did to guide me. She explained that her guidance primarily consisted in providing intuitive feelings about my life directions. In other words, she is that little voice in my ear—my internal direction and warning system. Evidently, we also work together often on the other side, when my physical body is asleep and I am astrally projecting, but these experiences are consciously remembered only as fragments of dreams.

In the years since our first meeting, whenever I go into a deep altered state and purposely seek out my guide, Neeta is always there waiting for me. I see her with my inner eyes and hear her with my inner ears.

Some people have suggested that this is just my imagination and I'm only talking or thinking to myself. That's certainly a possibility, but as with all subjective explorations, I have to judge by the results. Was the advice of value? Were the warnings reliable? Did the encouragement and support help me do a better job? The answer is always the same: Yes, yes, yes! Judging from hundreds of experiences, Neeta has greatly assisted me through her guidance. She's been extremely accurate in telling me about the future. And though she never directly tells me what to do, she points out potentials and cautions me about forthcoming conflicts.

For the past twelve years, before going out on stage to conduct a seminar or into a television studio for an interview, I have made it a point to always visit my spirit guide. I know it sounds corny, but these sessions are a lot like a coach's impassioned pregame speech to his team. She tells me such things as, "Our energy will be supporting you. The best answers will always surface as you draw upon lifetimes of awareness to respond intelligently and with love and compassion."

During these conversations I mentally sit in a chair beside Neeta. Off to the side are thousands of others —the people of Teotihuacan, with whom I share the dharma of communicating metaphysical concepts. While I ascend back into consciousness, I can hear them cheering. As a result I go out on stage feeling warm and self-assured.

Dharma is your duty to yourself and to society. It is usually best fulfilled by following your self-nature— what you are drawn to and do naturally and well. In fulfilling your purpose, you evolve spiritually. Of course you can always choose not to fulfill your dharma, but your spirit guide will attempt to keep you on the path.

Some metaphysicians call a primary guide a "lifetime guide." Those leaning toward Christian beliefs often perceive their unseen companions as "guardian angels." A question I'm often asked is, "Can you have more than one guide?" The answer appears to be yes, but you will have only one primary guide.

There are many reasons you might have more than one guide. I once worked with a woman who became increasingly involved with spiritual activities and service to others. She exceeded her life plan by advancing further than either she or her guide had expected she would. During some experimental hypnosis work we communicated directly with her guide, who explained that he had sought a "support guide" with more spiritual awareness who could better understand the transformations the woman was experiencing.

I'm also familiar with cases where the situation was reversed. Maybe an individual is out of control and really on the wrong path. Then his or her primary guide can ask for the assistance of a support guide who might have more expertise in dealing with strong resistance to spiritual growth.

How long a support guide remains present seems to vary with each individual. Often this second guide, too, stays close by for the rest of your earth life. I know of some cases where a deceased mate, relative, or close friend has become a support guide to the one they once loved on earth, but this supposedly cannot happen unless the discarnate entity is quite evolved and well beyond early fear-based emotions. If the entity were still capable of experiencing jealousy, for example, they could never be allowed to take on this role because they might interfere with the course of their loved one's continuing life on earth.

One afternoon, while Tara and I were meditating together in Sedona, Arizona, my wife first met her spirit guides. We were near the Boynton Canyon energy vortex in an area we perceive to have once been sacred to the Indians. Lying down in a smooth rock wash, we held hands, my right in Tara's left, and between our clasped hands we placed a favorite quartz crystal. Crystals are amplifiers and can intensify a subjective experience.

There was no specific purpose for the meditation other than to open to spiritual awareness. When we awakened, Tara excitedly told me about meeting her two guides. First her primary guide, Françoise, had appeared before her, and she was so happy-go-lucky in her communications that Tara had felt like laughing. Then Françoise introduced Tara's support guide, Abenda. Abenda was calm and very serious and explained that she had joined Françoise when Tara was twenty-one because my wife had been too free-spirited and reckless. Since Françoise herself was gregarious and free-spirited, she needed some assistance in providing Tara with grounding and direction.

The rest of Tara's meditation session was spent with her guides, who explained many things about the spirit world and our relationship. Since then my wife has communicated regularly with her unseen companions.

Though we had had many conversations about spirit guides, I'd never told Tara what Neeta looked like. Yet on a rough airplane flight during one of our seminar tours, Tara perfectly described her to me.

Concerned about our safety, since the plane was dipping wildly through stormy skies, Tara went into an altered state to talk with her guides. They told her there was no need to fear and explained that we were perfectly safe and had a lot of work to do before we were ready to cross over into spirit. Then Neeta appeared to Tara. She was dressed in tan leather, looking just as I've always visualized her. After she too reassured Tara as to our safety, she began to talk about me, and about how much she approved of the relationship Tara and I shared. It seems that Neeta and the tribe had participated in the decision that Tara would be the woman I would spend the rest of my life with. We had shared many lifetimes, including the Teotihuacan incarnation, and this bonding would be a reward. With her at my side, I would continue to do the work I was destined to accomplish, and she would become involved in her own metaphysical explorations.

Since that flight, Neeta has often appeared to Tara —usually to chat, sometimes to offer advice about me. Occasionally, when Tara is meditating, Neeta will join Françoise and Abenda and all three will begin communicating at once. "It can be a little overwhelming," my wife once said, after a lengthy session.

After direct communication with your spirit guides is established, one of the biggest mistakes you can make is to give them too much power. I've seen many people do this. You must always use your own judgment about advice you receive subjectively. As the guide of a hypnotized woman once told me, "Dying doesn't increase your intelligence!"

Also, be aware that a true spiritual guide will not use gutter language, will never scare you, and will never make you feel ill at ease.

Of course, they could always share some piece of knowledge that might disturb you. I recall a woman who was very upset with her guides because they didn't like the man she was seeing. "My guides are so negative," she said. "All they do is put down this wonderful new man I've been dating, so I'm not talking to them anymore." You've probably already guessed the outcome of this story. The new boyfriend stole several hundred dollars from the woman before disappearing, never to be heard from again.

The physical appearance of their guide is always a

concern of people in my seminars. Since there is neither male nor female on the other side, the guide will choose a "comfortable" appearance. This might be the way they looked in their last earth life, at what they considered to be an ideal age. It is also possible that your primary guide has never incarnated upon the earth, although these cases seem to be the exceptions. And it doesn't necessarily mean that the guide never experienced a physical incarnation, for there are millions of other realities.

Most metaphysicians, myself included, have found that an extremely high percentage of spirit guides are American Indians, Hindus, Egyptians, or Chinese. I have no explanation for this other than these races seem to personify wisdom. Maybe we are more likely to accept their guidance than we would that of, say, an ex-accountant from the Bronx.

In some cases, guides seem to prefer to appear as a light or illuminated energy. The light is usually white or blue, and often looks like it is moving. I usually think of deep blue or purple lights as indicating contact with a Master rather than with spirit guides.

A Master is a very highly evolved spirit that would be drawn to you to assist you in attaining spiritual awareness or to assist you in metaphysical service. You've heard the statement, "When the student is ready, the Master will appear." A Master has the ability to work with thousands of students, and comes and goes in your life, or works with you at night when you are asleep and out of body. Jesus and Buddha are Masters, but there are many others.

Getting back to spirit guides, you should be aware that you have the guides you deserve. One of the Universal Laws is the Divine Law of Attraction. In other words, where your attention goes, your energy flows . . . or, like attracts like. So you get the kind of guides that you have earned in your past. When I say past, I mean all of your past lives, the time between lives, and your present life up until this moment in time.

"My guide was a dullard!" a seminar participant once told me. "He didn't seem to have any energy or imagination. I think he was asleep at the switch! So I meditated and asked that someone else come in and replace him." He explained that every day for weeks he called out to the positive powers of the Universe, the concerned Masters and anyone else on the other side that might be of assistance. "Then one day they replaced the dullard and the new guy is great. We have a real rapport. He's a little old Chinese man who laughs funny."

This is the only case of its kind I'm aware of, and I'm not sure I accept it. But if you're unhappy with your guide and decide to try for a replacement, write and tell me about it.

I've explored a couple of cases where the entire family seems to have an "overguide." Each member of these families has his or her own primary guide, but a family overguide has also kept watch over generation after generation.

A young man in a Texas reincarnation seminar once stood up and told me that he thought the whole idea of guides was a stupid, self-created crutch to keep us from feeling alone! "I used to play the game of talking to my guides, but then one day I had a bad auto accident and was in the hospital for three weeks. If my guides were real, they certainly would have warned me about the accident!" he said.

"I disagree," I responded. "If the accident was necessary as karmic retribution, they would not have been allowed to tell you. To have informed you would mean they would have had to take on the karma themselves. Maybe the accident was the only way for you to learn a needed lesson about your driving before you killed yourself or someone else. Maybe the lesson was related to learning to accept the assistance of others. There is no way for me to know, but you can find out on your own. Maybe the accident was just cause-and-effect karma. In other words, you have been so negative in so many ways that you needed to *blow-off* that negativity, so you chose a fast, dramatic way to do it."

At the end of this chapter I'll provide a script to use in an altered-state-of-consciousness session where you can meet your own spiritual guide and ask your own questions. In preparing for that session, it's important not to have preconceptions about how your spirit guide will appear to you. Just as when you receive past-life impressions, it is different for everyone.

Instantaneous thought transference, or "thought language," is the primary way to receive information during meditation and to communicate with your guides. The air around you is filled with radio and TV messages, but you can't hear them until your set is turned on and tuned to the station you want to receive. The air around you is also filled with the voices of disembodied spirits, but you can't hear them until you become open to receive them. You hold the power to decide what messages you will receive and to what spiritual level you will be attuned.

If you use protective invocations, if you have a high level of awareness and if you sincerely desire to contact only highly evolved and loving entities, then mischievous or negative spirits cannot get through.

Using thought language in meditation is a matter of silently, subjectively sending out a thought, then listening for an internal answer which may be perceived as another thought, a feeling, or a fantasy-like visualization. Don't expect the voice of God to literally speak in your ear; instead, be alert for gentle intuitive feelings, ideas, and awarenesses. These may very well be directed from your own guides, Masters, or those whom you seek to contact. You'll soon sense when you are "in contact," and with a little practice, you'll be able to judge the validity of your experiences.

If an unseen voice uses bad language or tells you exactly what to do, immediately cease communication. Highly evolved souls won't command you; instead, they will gently guide you toward expanded awareness.

The more you develop this technique, the more effective it will become. Always be aware that you are in control in a meditation. If you feel uncomfortable in any way, just count yourself up from one to five, and say, "Wide awake!"

My altered-state-of-consciousness scripts always include the white light protection ritual. You can choose to intensify it by repeating it or adding to it. The higher your level of awareness, the less you need to use protection, but we all have "down" days when it would be easier for a low-level entity to come through. When I say low-level entity, I mean one of a number of earthbound spirits who remain in the lower astral planes, often unaware that they are dead, and desperately trying to cling to life.

The more peaceful, harmonious, and healthy you are, the easier it will be to communicate directly with your spirit guides, and the harder it will be for an undesirable entity to influence you.

Your primary guide is particularly concerned about your needs and will always assist you, whether you ask for help or not. But if you openly ask for assistance, they can do so much more. Frequently, in sessions with Neeta, I have asked for assistance on a particular problem but haven't necessarily received my answers immediately. The awareness might come in a dream, or I might awaken in the morning with the answer in my mind.

I also like to point out that *everything* speaks to you, if you are open enough to listen and to observe. A sign by the road, a passage in a book, or a line in a song might be exactly what would most benefit you in regard to your current need or conflict. Finding a heart-shaped stone might be a way for your unseen companions to communicate their presence, or to let you know you are loved.

Always remember to trust your instincts; do not expect your guides to make decisions for you. A guide cannot tell you what to do; he can show you alternatives and offer general awareness, but the final decision will always be up to you. Also, after each session with your guides, be sure to thank them for sharing their wisdom and express your positive feelings toward them.

Spirit Guide Meditation Script

(Insert the induction provided in the last chapter.) "In my superconscious mind lies an awareness of ultimate truth and the totality. Within my subconscious mind lies an awareness of everything that has ever happened to me throughout all time. On a superconscious level I am aware of how all the people in my life relate to my past and of the involved karmic interaction that I have set as a path for learning and to fulfill my dharma. I am also aware of time spent on the other side between lifetimes and of my spirit guides who are even now assisting me in accomplishing the growth I so desire.

"My primary guide has been with me since birth, always assisting me in the fulfillment of my personal mission. Love is the power behind the guidance, and I am aware that it is I who have asked my guide for this direction.

"And it is now time to make contact with my

primary spiritual guide so that we can directly communicate about my life and the unseen realms. I will begin by perceiving my guide's primary name. There are many names in many languages—some which I have never heard spoken and many languages I have never even heard of—so I will not prejudge what I receive. I will simply allow the letters of my guide's name to come into my mind, one letter at a time. First letter . . . second letter . . . third letter . . . fourth letter . . . fifth letter . . . and if there are additional letters, allow them to come in now. *(Pause. When you have perceived the name, say it over and over, silently in your mind. If the name sounds unusual, you may discover—with a little research—that it is common in another language or an ancient culture.)*

"And I now want to perceive exactly what my guide looks like, so on the count of three he or she will mentally appear before me. I will trust my impressions as I have never trusted before. Number one, I'm opening and asking my guide to appear before me. Number two, I beseech you to be with me now. Number three. *(Pause. Perceive your guide before you. If necessary, begin with the feet and allow them to form. Then slowly move up and notice the details, a few at a time. Is your guide male or female? If necessary, choose what seems most correct. How old does he or she appear to you? What about hair color and style? Perceive your guide's clothing.)*

"All right, I am now going to use thought language to communicate directly with my guide." *(Pause. If you have prerecorded this session, leave several minutes of blank tape here to ask questions and receive answers.)*

"All right, I am now interested in my guide's past lives, especially if the two of us have shared incarnations. Let this awareness come in the form of visual impressions and thought language. *(Pause.)*

"And I'd now like to discuss with my guide the areas of my life that I need to change if I desire to accomplish my mission and evolve spiritually. *(Pause.)*

"I would now like to discuss with my guide how I can best serve this planet. What can I do to assist others and serve the planet? *(Pause. Say your final good-byes, or ask more questions. Thank your guides. Use the awaken script to return to full beta consciousness.)*

The next time you desire to meet your guide, just go into an altered state and call out to your guide, asking him to join you.

CHAPTER

4

Past Lives

Helen Kuhlmann, Baton Rouge, LA: "I am sixty-one years old. Throughout most of my adult life, I've suffered with throat problems. At irregular intervals, for no apparent reason, I would begin to choke. My throat would itch horribly until tears ran down my face. Strangely, this choking would only affect one side of my throat at a time, with only one eye shedding tears.

"The choking was so severe that had both sides been affected at once, I would not have been able to breathe. After several painful minutes, the episode would end . . . until the next time. The medical profession could offer no help.

"During Easter 1986, I attended your psychic seminar in Sedona, Arizona. In the group back-to-the-cause regression, I vividly experienced being a handsome youth in my twenties, in Missouri. The year was 1889. When you directed us to the death experience, I relived being falsely accused of some sexual behavior by a jealous woman. Without judge or jury, I was sentenced to stand behind a wagon, a rope knotted around my neck. When the horses were whipped forward, I was strangled to death.

"In the regression, I imagined my throat closing and I began to cry. Then I heard a clear message: 'You can now release this!' I did and the choking stopped and has not returned for over two years.

"Oh yes, the jealous woman is my daughter in this lifetime and we have a rocky relationship at best. I have not shared this with her."

Barbara J. Litchfield, Hillsboro, NJ: "I have had several past-life regression experiences that not only answered questions I had about certain situations in my life but changed my attitudes toward them as well. The regressions evolved quite naturally while I was in meditation. Since I have been meditating over a long period of time, the sessions grew from seeing a speck of light to seeing fluid colors. At other times, I would see flashes of pictures, until finally entire scenes would unfold before my mind's eye.

"At the time I began experiencing past-life regressions, I was at a point in my life when my focus was on money: why wasn't I making any, how come I could not hold on to what little I had, why did I detest any type of banking activity, what skills did I have to help me earn more money, etc. I leave 90 percent of our finances to my husband to handle. Although I've tried, I've never been able to force myself to get into budgeting, accounting, and banking.

"In meditation, I asked my Higher Self to show me why money was so troublesome to me. A white picket fence then came into focus. It surrounded a well-kept Victorian home located at the end of town that I immediately knew was my home. A man came out the front door. As I watched, I knew intuitively that the man was me. He was well groomed, with long side-burns, brown hair, and wire-rimmed glasses, and wore a three-piece suit. He worked for the bank, and I understood that he was popular with the ladies. As he approached the gate, three men came up to him in the street; I had the impression they were farmers from the way they were dressed. They began discussing the reasons they had to borrow money from the bank. The bank had already refused their request.

"The discussion became very heated. Then one of the farmers took out a gun and shot the banker in the left temple. When this happened, my consciousness fused with the banker. I saw a red aura and knew it was my own blood. For a moment, I felt panic and the fear of death, then darkness settled in.

"Maybe the regression explains why I detest banking and dealing with money. I subconsciously fear that involvement with money could lead to another terrible experience.

"I have experienced many other past lives while in meditation, but on another occasion while in meditation, I came back to this banker's life. I was asking about my relationship with my seven-year-old son, Jonathan. As much as I love him, he does things that truly annoy and aggravate me. I'm sure this is true of all children to some extent, but my four-year-old son, Christopher, does the same things Jonathan does and I'm not bothered.

"When I asked my Higher Self why, I saw myself as the banker again, walking down the dirt street of the town. A carriage pulled up in front of me and a woman got out, handing me a three-year-old child. The woman said she could no longer take care of the child. I was left holding this little girl, who didn't even know me. Her name was Penelope and I knew I was her biological father. To summarize the rest of the story, I wasn't about to take care of the girl alone. Acknowledging my responsibility, but without getting emotionally involved, I sent her away to live with an elderly aunt. In effect, I got rid of her.

"Today, this child is my son Jonathan and I can understand why our relationship is difficult at times. I'm certain that some of his feelings of neglect from the previous lifetime have carried over into this one. Since discovering the nature of our relationship, I have increased my involvement in all his school and social activities. We visit zoos, museums, parks, go camping and swimming, and we chat, read, and watch TV together. I'm enjoying it! I feel compelled to be there for him and perhaps make amends for that lifetime of neglect."

Mary L. Ayala, Toledo, OH: "While attending your seminar in Cleveland, Ohio, I experienced two vivid past-life regressions. I was amazed to have gotten anything because I have never been regressed and I just assumed I wouldn't be a good hypnotic subject."

(Mary describes a lifetime which explains a deep friendship and her love for Italy, where she lives for six months out of every year. She then goes on to describe an incarnation related to her current weight problem.)

"My first impressions were of a beautiful summer day; I saw myself as a fifteen- or sixteen-year-old girl wearing a blue dress with a white collar, and a white cap that fit close to the head. I had long, honey-colored hair worn straight and tucked up under the hat. My figure was narrow-waisted with ample bust and hips.

"I had the feeling this girl was quite simple as I watched her walk through the pasture. In the barn I could even smell the cow I/she leaned up against as it turned and nuzzled me. As I turned and walked through the barnyard, mud splattered my wooden shoes. Suddenly, appearing in the doorway of the chicken coop was a man, a malevolent figure with white skin and glaring black eyes. I cringed and scurried past him to get into the house; his hatred for me was almost tangible.

"Then vivid images of sexual abuse began to form. I saw how he raped and beat me horribly, saying, 'You're fat and ugly!' The abuse was nonstop, night and day. He starved me, so whenever he wasn't around, I ate frantically. I was always hungry and was afraid I would starve to death. At this point, a voice told me this is the reason I cannot control my eating in this life whenever I feel stressed or threatened.

"I eventually lost my mind from the continuous abuse. Death followed. The abuser in that life was my mother-in-law in my present life. We hated each other from the moment our eyes met twenty-eight years ago. She made my life as hellish as she could, but this time I won. When she died, I surprised myself by wishing her well. I don't hate her anymore. Hopefully, I'll never have to meet her again.

"I'm currently using your weight-control program and am trying to soothe the scared simpleton who still lives inside me and who wants to eat every time my husband is abrupt or less than loving, which I feel is most of the time. I may not succeed in this lifetime, but I feel so much better knowing why I am the way I am."

Jane W. Chartrand, Shelbyville, TN: "I am an only child, a fact that was devastating to me when I was growing up. My parents hadn't wanted children; I was quite an unpleasant surprise, for they were rather old to be starting a family. My childhood was very unhappy; my mother mistreated me physically and emotionally, but this never deterred me from wanting a large family of my own. In three past-life regressions, I've experienced being an only child—this might explain my desire for a large family.

"I married at twenty and our first child was born a year later. When it became apparent that I couldn't have any more, we adopted seven children in the next eighteen years. Denise, the child I am writing about, is our third. We adopted her when she was one year old. Following her adoption, I was plagued with the feeling that we wouldn't see her grow up. I didn't know whether we would lose her to an illness, an accident, or whatever, but the feeling persisted for many years. My husband and I were confused and very worried because I seem to have a pretty good intuitive sense about things. As Denise approached her teens, the feeling gradually disappeared until it was all but forgotten.

"Then, while I was using one of your regression tapes, I experienced being a nineteen-year-old woman living in London in the 1800s. My parents were dead and I was raising my six-year-old sister. I earned my living as a seamstress, working long, hard hours. In the regression, my sister and I were walking along a cobblestone sidewalk, and she was admiring a small ball I had given her for Christmas. As I looked down at her, I realized she was Denise in my present life. As we walked, the ball got away from her and rolled into the street. She ran after it and was killed by a fast approaching horse and buggy.

"A week or so later, I mentioned the regression experience to my husband and he said, 'That must explain why you thought something was going to happen to Denise when she was little.' It hit me like a load of bricks—I had completely put that feeling out of my mind until he mentioned it."

Everyone on this planet has past-life memories locked away in the subconscious mind. These memories are affecting you right now. You are the living result of all your past programming from all of your lifetimes.

Karma is the supreme Universal Law. It is the very basis of reality. When I ask metaphysical audiences how many of them believe in karma, they all raise their hand, yet few people live their lives as if they totally accept the idea. Maybe they don't understand the full implications. Once you do, you make a lot of important changes in the way you think and the way you live.

Karma either is or it isn't . . . there is no halfway karmic reality. Karma is either the force behind everything in your life, or it is nothing. This is either a random universe and our life is soulless and meaningless, or there is a *plan behind all this* . . . *a meaning to life.* And, if there is a plan, then it would follow that an Intelligence is behind the plan and justice has to be a part of it all.

Look around you. Where is the justification for the misery and inequality in the world? How can you justify millions of starving people . . . wars . . . victims of senseless crimes? Why is it that loving parents may lose their child in a terrible accident while neglectful and abusive parents raise their child to adulthood? How can you justify the criminals and dope dealers who get ahead financially while an honest man toils for his family and never has an extra dime? How can you explain all the misery and suffering in the world?

Reincarnation and karma can explain it all. And there is no other philosophy or religion that can. Christianity certainly can't . . . not in the context of one lifetime.

To make that perfectly clear, let's explore a hypothetical situation: Two little girls are both born on the same day. The first is born crippled, into miserable circumstances—a home without love in an area of extreme poverty. The second little girl is born healthy, to loving parents who are financially well off. The crippled girl lives with daily physical and emotional suffering and dies a very painful death at an early age. The second little girl has a beautiful life and grows up to have a good marriage, a fulfilling career, and children of her own. She dies a peaceful death as an elderly woman.

How is the life of misery justified? The Bible infers that you'll "reap your reward in heaven." But what about the girl who had the good life? Does she find a lesser reward? Obviously, it doesn't work. But karma explains it all!

Let's theorize about the karma of the little girl who experienced the miserable life: Suppose, in a previous life, she was a male soldier who enjoyed watching the suffering of enemy prisoners, perhaps even tortured them. Then, in another lifetime, she was a mother who abandoned her child. Before being born into her current lifetime, she spent some time on the other side reflecting about those lifetimes and said to herself, "I'm going into this lifetime and get those two debts cleared up fast. Obviously, I need to experience suffering to better understand it, so I'll be born with a painful, crippling affliction. I need to directly experience the anguish of parental rejection, so I will be born to unloving parents. Then, I'll die painfully at the age of fifteen and the karma will be balanced."

Having made this decision while in spirit on the other side, she seeks parents with a karmic configuration that fits her need. Perhaps they need to have a child born to them who has these physical problems and circumstances. Ideally, parents would be found with whom the girl had already shared a background of earthly incarnations.

Once this is all put together, the parents are born; then later, the child is born and the learning and suffering begins. If you knew this child personally, you were probably very upset by it all. It made your heart very sad to see this child suffer and you were disgusted by the parents because they were so uncaring and negligent.

But the moment this child died and found herself on the other side, she said, "Whew! Well, that balanced that and that . . . now I can get on with some more creative and spiritual evolution."

Obviously, I am oversimplifying the concept, but you see the point. Karma explains everything. That is why it is part of most of the world's religions. It was a tenet of early Christianity, too, but was eliminated from church doctrine by decree of the Second Council of Constantinople in A.D. 553.

Let's go back to the very basics in understanding reincarnation and karma . . . and I'll cover the points that even those who accept the idea often prefer to forget. Remember, *karma either is or it isn't.* There is no halfway plan. There is no halfway justice. Karma is absolutely everything or it is nothing, and there is no meaning to life. Either accept karma or reject karma, but don't waste your time taking a position somewhere in between.

Karma is cause and effect. Pick up a stone and throw it into a small pond. You and the stone are the cause; the splash and the ripples are the effect. Your action disturbs the harmony of the pond. The ripples flow out and back, out and back until, due to the physical law of "dissipation of energy," the pond eventually returns to its original state of tranquillity.

Similarly, all your thoughts and actions disturb the balanced harmony of the universe. Everything you do creates vibrations that flow out and back upon you until, through your lifetimes, your karma is eventually balanced and you are harmonious once again.

One principle to keep in mind is that karma will

react upon you with the same force that you established when setting it into motion. And karma is constantly in motion, acting on every level of your body and mind. Everything you *think, feel* or *do* creates or erases karma. And this includes the *motive, intent,* and *desire* behind every thought and action.

If an act is preceded by intention, then karma results. An example of a physical act would be the giving of a gift; a verbal act would be lying. Such acts are almost always motivated by desire or dislike, which signify intention. Every thought and action generates energy and leaves an impression or residue in your mind that at some later time will produce a consequence.

I'll come back to this concept in a moment, but first, let's explore another one: In addition to your birth karma, you create new karma every day, both good and bad. *And,* you pay it off every day. Most of this is simple cause and effect balancing karma. According to brain/mind medical research, your mind operates like a computer. And since it operates like a computer, computer jargon is appropriate in understanding how we program ourselves on a daily basis. The data processing term that best applies is "G.I.G.O.," which means "garbage in, garbage out." If you incorrectly program your computer with "garbage" in the form of negative thought, you'll automatically generate negativity that will have to be experienced in your life.

If the subconscious were to receive no new programming, it would continue to operate on past input. This, of course, cannot happen, for you are constantly feeding new programming or data into your subconscious mind—your computer. Every thought programs the computer. Thus, if you are thinking more negatively than positively, you are programming your computer in the wrong way. *You create your own reality or karma with your thoughts.*

Many people have no idea how negatively they think. If you climb out of bed cursing the alarm clock, grouch through breakfast, get upset about the weather and the heavy traffic on the freeway and whine about how much you dislike your job, and on and on throughout the day, you are literally creating a worse reality for yourself. Because you are thinking more negative thoughts than positive during the day, there is simply no way you could be creating anything but a negative reality. With all that negative programming in your computer, how could it do anything but create the programmed result—more negativity!

KARMA! Everything you *think, feel,* and *do* creates or erases karma. And this includes the *motive, intent,* and *desire* behind every thought and action. Think about that! It really affects the way you are generating your personal karmic debits and credits. Do you help someone out of true compassion, or because when you do, you get your own ego pumped about what a good person you are, or you feel it is the right thing to do, or you're concerned about what the other people in your office might think if you don't give to the charity drive? Or because you want a write-off on your tax return?

Why you do what you do is just as important as *what* you do in your life from a karmic perspective. The unerring law of karma is always adjusting and balancing as a result of your *free choices,* which result in the effects you experience. Every condition in your current life is the result of karma you have generated up to this very moment. Your body, your weight, your health are all karmic. Your monetary success or lack of success . . . everything in your life is karmic.

As a result of my work in this field, I am convinced that neither God nor the Lords of Karma bestow your suffering upon you. It is *your* decision and *yours alone* to tackle the opportunities you are experiencing in your life. You and you alone are responsible for absolutely everything that has ever happened to you. You are your own judge and jury. In your Higher Mind, you are fully aware that in order to progress, you must learn. And the fastest way to learn is by directly experiencing the actual consequences of your own actions.

Therefore, if you and you alone are responsible for absolutely everything that has ever happened to you, then there is no one to blame for anything that has ever happened to you. *There is no one to blame for anything!* The concept of blame is totally incompatible with reincarnation and karma. There are no victims. Your ex-mate with whom you had such a hard time; the partner who ripped you off; the in-laws you hate; your sadistic boss; the guy who raped you when you were only twelve; the burglars who robbed your house . . . you created them all because you needed to balance karma and you wanted to test yourself.

Take a moment and think back on your life. Think about everyone in your past who really made life difficult for you. In actuality, these were the people who really helped you the most in accomplishing your goal of spiritual evolution. They helped you balance your karma. Each one was a test you created to determine how well you are progressing in attaining a perspective of unconditional love.

It is easy to tell whether you are passing or failing your own tests. If you respond with love, positive thoughts, and compassion, you are probably passing the test. If you respond with negativity and blame, you are probably failing. And if you choose to fail, that is all right . . . you'll just have to come back and try it again. If neither you nor the person causing you problems learns this time, you will come back together in a future life and get another opportunity. If one learns and the other doesn't, the one who learns has resolved his or her karma. The one who didn't will find someone else with a similar karmic configuration and they will come together to test themselves in the future.

Often in balancing karma, you don't even have to wait for the next lifetime for a new opportunity to arise. We have all observed in others—and probably in ourselves as well—recurring, undesirable patterns. This is a situation of learning through *pain* until we finally "get it" intuitively, once and for all, that what we are doing doesn't work.

You were born with a package of karma that you desired to experience. From a spiritual perspective, if you are testing yourself, it is only your reactions to the experiences that are important.

When we are on the other side in spirit preparing to enter into a lifetime, I think we are very brave.

For instance, you may say to yourself, "Okay, I think I'm ready to test myself in another relationship with Donald. If he's willing, we'll fall in love when I'm twenty-two. We'll get married a year later. We'll have three children, and right about the time the third child is born, when I'm thirty-two, Donald will begin to ignore me and start having affairs with other women. He'll divorce me when I'm thirty-four. This time, because I owe Don one in this area, I'll respond with love and understanding and emotionally support him."

Actually the events wouldn't be predestined to this degree, for you always have the free will to choose whether you will interject new wisdom and under-standing into the situation. And what if both parties respond without added enlightenment? You were very brave and aware over there on the other side. Now comes the reality. But what do you do? You scream and threaten and blame. You hire a hotshot lawyer who socks it to Donald financially for the rest of his days. You and Donald now hate each other. This is another example of learning through pain. You and Don can plan to return for another round in the year 2046.

Actually, there is no such thing as failing your own karmic test. If you fell off your bicycle nine times before you finally learned to ride on your tenth attempt, the nine failures were actually small successes which eventually led to the ultimate success. How many times you fall before reaching your goal is up to you.

In addition to our day-to-day karma, there is karma yet unknown to you. It is stored up from the past, waiting for a suitable opportunity to discharge itself. This could happen later in this life or in your next life or in a lifetime after that. Not everything can be balanced in one lifetime.

The good news is, the Law of Grace supersedes the Law of Karma. This means that if you give love, grace, and mercy, you will receive the same in return. All your positive and loving thoughts and actions go to cancel out your stored-up bad karma. And, since this is so, it is probably time for you to begin to think about how you can be more positive, loving, and compassionate, and how you can support good works and serve this planet, if only to reduce the amount of undesirable karma that you have awaiting you in the future.

Also, wisdom erases karma, and we can mitigate karmic burdens through awareness. The techniques of past-life therapy and regression therapy are often useful shortcuts in doing this. In the past, we've learned through pain. In other words, we've learned not to touch hot stoves because, by touching them, we burn our fingers. After experiencing the pain of touching so many hot stoves, we realize, once and for all, that it's something we should avoid. Most of us begin to discover our karmic lessons the same way.

When we choose to approach them through wisdom, though, we accept what we need to learn by becoming aware of the lesson, forgiving ourselves and letting go of it. Karma simply seeks to restore your disturbed equilibrium. You can do it the hard way through pain, or the easy way through wisdom and grace.

Of course, to learn through wisdom you must *forgive yourself.* Since you are your own judge and jury, it is up to you to forgive yourself. The only problem is that you will not do this unless you feel that the karma is totally balanced or the lesson learned. You can't fool yourself in this area. To truly forgive yourself, you must know on every level of your body and mind that you will never forget again.

If you are not yet able to forgive yourself to this degree, you must decide what you can do to achieve this desired level of self-forgiveness. Can you do something symbolic to show that you have learned?

In working with people in past-life therapy, I've found that what I call "symbolic restitution" can be very powerful. As an example, I'll share the case of a man who suffered severe back problems most of his adult life. Medically, nothing was found to be wrong with him. In hypnotically induced past-life regression, he relived a past life as a soldier in World War I. During battle, an artillery shell exploded near him, sending shrapnel into his back. He died slowly, in great pain, after several days, with much bitterness toward the enemy for his early, senseless death.

With this knowledge revealed, he decided to become actively involved in the peace movement. This was four years ago, and since then, he has strongly supported world peace organizations. And his back is slowly improving.

In another case, a woman with a long history of relationship problems relived a recent past life as a man who mistreated, raped, and beat many women. As a form of symbolic restitution, the woman began volunteering her time to assist in a clinic for battered women. In this way, she will quickly attain, through wisdom, an awareness of the pain caused by such actions. Remember, the purpose of karma is learning, and we have the ability to accelerate the learning.

To make these ideas easier to communicate, I have been using the terms "bad" and "good," which isn't in keeping with metaphysical thought. It would be much more appropriate to use the words "harmony" and "disharmony." Your positive, loving thoughts and actions generate harmony. Your negative, fear-based thoughts and actions generate disharmony. Disharmony obviously generates the kind of karma that will have to be balanced in the future.

There is only one cause of disharmony and that is *fear*—all the fear-based emotions. We are all here on earth because we desire to evolve spiritually. We have karma to resolve and the way to do it is to let go of fear and express unconditional love.

DISCOVER YOUR OWN PAST LIVES

Combining the induction provided in the last chapter of this book, the awareness I've already shared, and the information I'll now provide, you can safely, easily, and effectively recall your own past lives. I would suggest that you begin with a warm-up regression session. I'll provide a script with notations. Tape-record it, memorize it, paraphrase it, or have someone else ask the questions once you've used the induction technique to put yourself into an altered state of consciousness.

Warm-up Regression Script

(Following induction) "In the memory banks of my subconscious mind there is a memory of everything that has ever happened to me in this life I am now living, or in any of my past lives. Every thought, every spoken word, every deed from every lifetime I have ever lived is recorded in these memory banks and I am now going to allow some of these subconscious memories to filter down out of the subconscious and into my conscious mind where I can look at them once again. I am now going to begin to move backward in time to one of my previous incarnations. My superconscious mind will choose a lifetime that will be of value for me to reexamine at this time. In a moment I will create a vivid mental impression of a tunnel to my own past, and I will count backward from five to one. As I count, I will see myself moving through the tunnel into my past, and on the count of one, I will step out of the end of the tunnel and perceive myself at the age of fifteen in a previous lifetime."

(Pause and mentally create a vivid impression of any kind of tunnel that is pleasing to you. It will serve as a "mental bridge" between the present and the past. Imagine yourself stepping into it and proceed.)

"And I'm now stepping into the tunnel . . . number five, I'm moving backward in time. I feel myself moving through the tunnel into my past . . . and at the end of the tunnel, I can see a light. I'm moving toward the light. On the count of one, I'll be there. On the count of one, I'll step out of the end of the tunnel and see myself at the age of fifteen in another time and another place. Number four . . . moving through time

. . . allowing it to happen . . . I can feel it happening . . . and I'm picking up speed as I move toward the light at the end of the tunnel. Number three . . . I'm moving closer and closer and closer to the light at the end of the tunnel . . . closer to seeing myself in my own past life at the age of fifteen. Number two . . . I'm getting very close now . . . I'm almost there . . . I can feel it happening . . . On the next count, I will perceive myself at the age of fifteen in a previous lifetime. Number one . . . I am now there. I am fifteen years of age."

(Even if you are not yet visualizing vividly, respond to the following questions with answers that seem correct. The initial "door opening" questions can be answered one way or another, and it is very important that you go ahead and "make up" the answers if need be. If you will just trust yourself enough to make up responses and visualizations, your subconscious seems to get the idea and soon you'll realize that the situation just seems to be appearing in your mind or before your inner eyes without effort or guidance.)

"Am I outdoors or indoors?" *(Pause. You have to be one or the other! If you're outdoors, you'll find yourself in a particular environment—by the sea, in the mountains, on the prairie, in a town or city. If you're indoors, you'll find yourself within an enclosure of a particular size. How high is the ceiling? What is the floor made of? Are there any doors or windows? Furnishings? If necessary, go ahead and make up the environment.)*

"Is there anyone else here with me or am I alone?" *(Pause)* "Am I male or female?" *(Pause)* "What am I wearing on my feet?" *(Pause. This question often triggers regressive impressions. Trust the first impression you receive and let it unfold: boots, shoes, sandals, moccasins, or are you barefoot?)*

"All right, now on the count of three I am going to

step outside of myself and perceive what I look like. I know if I'm male or female and what I'm wearing on my feet. . . . Number one, number two, number three. *(Pause and perceive everything about yourself: What color is your hair and how is it worn? How are you dressed? Perceive the style of your attire, the fabric or material—everything!)*

"All right, now on the count of three, I am going to move forward in time to something important that happens in my future. I'm growing older, and on the count of three, vivid impressions of an important event will begin to form. Number one, number two, number three."

(It is important to always progress yourself forward in time by event as opposed to an exacting time frame. If you were to say, "I now move forward in time two years," you could have died during the time and thus be confused or fearful upon finding yourself on the astral plane.)

"What is the year I now find myself experiencing?" *(If the year isn't immediately apparent, trust the numbers as they come into your mind one at a time.)* The first number of the year? Second number? Third number? And if there is a fourth number I'll perceive it now." *(Pause)* "Is that B.C. or A.D.?" *(Pause. Now do the same thing with the country or geographical area— if necessary, one letter at a time.)*

"All right, I will now move in time to a situation in which I find myself together with the one other person in this lifetime who is more important to me than any other. Number one, number two, number three." *(Pause)*

"And now I will perceive impressions from this life that relate to what I do for a career, occupation, or the primary way I spend my time. One, two, three." *(Pause)*

"All right, I am now going to open to impressions

which will assist me in attaining a karmic overview of this lifetime. One, two, three." *(Pause)*

(Insert any other questions you desire. The following "Death Experience" and "Spirit Crossover" could be inserted before ending with the "Return to the Present" and "Awakening.")

Death Experience Script

"On the count of three, *and not before the count of three,* I am going to move forward to the very last day of my life in the incarnation I am now examining. I will not have died, I will not have crossed over into spirit, but on the count of three, it will be the last day of my life in this past lifetime. As an absolute command, I will feel no pain and no emotion, and I will experience this situation objectively, only as an observer."

Spirit Crossover Script

"On the count of three, without pain and without emotion, I will re-experience this past life cross over into spirit. On the count of three, it will be a few moments after experiencing physical death in the previous incarnation I am now examining. One, two, three." *(Pause)*

"I am now in spirit and I will perceive the environment I find myself within. Look around. Allow feeling impressions to come in. Can I see the physical body I just left? If so, where am I in relationship to the body? *(75 percent will be floating above it.)* Do I sense any colors or sounds? Do I feel or see or sense anyone else here with me? *(If yes, ask if anything is being communicated to you.)* All right, let's move forward in time until there is contact of some kind, or until something happens. One, two, three." *(You will rarely be able to explore much deeper into the afterlife, but it is worth a try.)*

Return to the Present Script

"All right, I am going to let go of this and return to the present time on the count of three. I'll remain in a deep, altered state of consciousness, but on the count of three I'll be back in *(year and city)* . . . and as an absolute command, I will remember everything about this past lifetime. One, two, three."

Awakening Script

"In just a moment I am going to awaken to full beta consciousness, feeling as if I've had a nice, refreshing nap. My head will be clear, and I'll be thinking and acting with calm self-assurance, feeling glad to be alive, and at peace with myself, the world, and everyone in it. On the count of five, I will open my eyes and be wide awake, feeling good. Number one, coming on up now and I sense an expanding spiritual light within. Number two, coming on up and at peace with all life. Number three, coming on up and I sense internal balance and harmony. Number four, I now recall the situation and the room. Number five, wide awake, wide awake!"

If I am conducting a seminar in which I use a variation of this "Warm-up Regression," there are always a few people who complain, "I didn't get anything!"

I ask, "Did you make it up to get it started, like I told you to?"

"No, I didn't want to do that," they reply. In other words, they wanted the past-life regression impressions to appear in their head the way they wanted them to appear. If the initial experience didn't match their expectations, they refused to play.

Subjective impressions are different for everyone. Even if you think you are making it up, it is very likely that you are making up real things. Or, if you are making it up, your subconscious will get the idea, kick in, and the real impressions will start to flow. As I have already explained, I always feel I am making it up, but research has proved me accurate again and again. The same thing is true of the hundreds of people I've individually regressed. At the time of the regression, don't worry whether it is real or not— you'll have plenty of time for that once you awaken and can do follow-up research.

To receive past-life impressions, you have to trust yourself! Once you've experienced the "Warm-Up Regression," you'll probably want to skip the initial segment in which you see yourself as the fifteen-year-old and get right to the lifetime experiences that are affecting you now.

The following script, "Back to the Cause," is basic to past-life therapy. It takes you back to the cause of any situation you desire to explore. If you were to go into therapy with a psychiatrist or psychologist, chances are the mental health professional would initially seek to understand the cause of your problems. He knows that with this awareness, he can help you to help yourself faster and more effectively. Psychiatrists and psychologists claim they only uncover the cause of their patients' problems about half the time. Of course they rarely include past-life explorations in their therapy. I think it is interesting to note that in cases I have researched, about half the time the problem originated in a past life. The other half will be (1) childhood incidents (forgotten and remembered), (2) incidents that you didn't realize were "cause events" because they didn't seem that important at the time (forgotten and remembered), (3) a series of interrelated incidents (forgotten and remembered).

Everything you feel about everything goes back to past programming. The back to the cause regression can be used to uncover any and all programming, positive and negative: "Why have I always been able to draw so well?" "Why did my husband and I feel instantly attracted?" "Why can't I take responsibility without experiencing anxiety?" "Why do I get along well with one sister and always fight with the other?" "Why am I so attracted to metaphysical concepts?" "Why have I made myself sick?"

Back to the Cause Regression

(Induction) "And I am now relaxed and at ease and open to awareness that will assist me to rise above my karma and evolve spiritually. I am ready to explore the cause of something in my life I desire to know more about. In my subconscious mind are the memories of everything that has ever happened to me—every thought, every spoken word, every deed is recorded in the memory banks of my mind. It is time to allow this forgotten awareness to surface, so I may better understand that which influences, restricts, or motivates me in the present.

"All right, I am now going to concentrate on the situation I intend to investigate through regression. I'll dwell upon it. I'll see the situation in my mind and live it once again as a fantasy, so that I communicate what I want to explore to my subconscious mind."

(Spend at least thirty seconds concentrating upon what you want to investigate.)

"All right, now in just a moment I am going to direct myself back into the past. I may go back to an earlier time in my present life, or I may return to an event that transpired in a previous incarnation. I am going to count backward from five to one as I move through the tunnel to my own past. On the count of one, I will step out of the end of the tunnel and begin to perceive vivid impressions from my past that relate to the cause of this situation."

(Visualize the tunnel and count backward. Once you step out of the end of the tunnel, if impressions don't begin to form on their own, ask yourself some of the basic questions to get them going: "Am I outdoors or indoors?" "What am I wearing on my feet?" etc.)

(Take as long as you need to explore the initial impressions of the cause event. If you have made a tape, leave at least two minutes of silent time to receive impressions.)

"All right, now let go of this. It's time to explore this situation in more detail from other perspectives. I want to attain a karmic overview of the situation. New impressions are now forming, which will assist me to fully understand everything of importance about it."

(Pause. It could be that the cause is actually a series of events and you'll need to direct yourself through many situations to uncover a more complete picture of what happened.)

(You might want to explore the year, the country or geographical area, and your career/occupation/primary way of spending time.)

"All right, I am now interested in the other people involved with me in this situation—the people in my past life and how they relate to my present incarnation. I have the ability to perceive impressions or awareness that will assist me in fully understanding how the past relates to the present."

(Pause. Remember, although you are receiving impressions from your subconscious mind, your conscious mind is still aware of what is going on and may be able

to help you access the higher understanding of your superconscious. If you are experiencing a past life, for example, ask yourself, "Who is the blacksmith in my current life?" If you receive an immediate, strong feeling, inner knowing or visualization of someone you currently know, the two of you probably have interactive karma.)

"All right, now I want to perceive very strong impressions about how to rise above this karma *(if you are exploring the cause of a negative situation).* Is the karma already nearly balanced? Have I almost learned so that I can let go of this effect? What can I do to rise above this karma? It will amount to *self-forgiveness,* but to truly forgive myself, I must now—on every level of my body and mind—know that I will never, ever forget the lesson again. If I am not yet able to forgive myself to that degree, what can I do to cleanse myself, to achieve this desired level of self-forgiveness? Can I do something symbolic to show that I have learned? Can I assist others as a form of restitution? Let the impressions come in now."

(As an example, a woman who couldn't have a baby found that she had abandoned a child in the 1800s. She still couldn't forgive herself enough to allow herself to get pregnant, so she began working as a volunteer in a children's hospital as restitution to accelerate the karmic process of self-forgiveness.)

(Return to the Present script)

"In a few moments I am going to awaken, but before I do I want to remind myself that wisdom erases karma, and the Law of Grace supersedes the Law of Karma. Karma can be experienced to the letter of the law or in mercy and grace. I now go out of my way to show mercy, grace and love, knowing I will receive the same in return. I seek to let go of all fear-based emotions and to express unconditional love in every area of my life. As it is above, so it is below. I ask these things, I beseech it, I mark it and so it is." *(Awaken script)*

The Life Most Affecting Your Current Life Script

(Induction) "In this session I am going to explore the one past lifetime that is most affecting my current life. I am aware that many past lives are affecting my current life. I am aware that many past lives are affecting me, but there is one life that is affecting me more than any other. I will begin this experience by perceiving an important or clarifying situation that took place during this important life."

(Travel back through the time tunnel to the past life and pause to allow time for the initial impressions to emerge.) "All right, I want to remember everything I am now experiencing, but it is time to move on and experience this lifetime in more detail and from other perspectives. New impressions are beginning to come in now." *(Pause. Next questions might be the year and country.)*

"All right, it's now time to let go of this and allow impressions to flow into my mind relating to my occupation, trade, or the primary way I spent my time in this incarnation I am now examining. *(Pause.)*

"And now, there is one other person who is more important to me than any other in this lifetime. Impressions now begin to come in that will assist me to understand the relationship we shared." *(Pause.)*

(You might want to insert this if you prerecord a tape.) "All right, I will continue to remember everything I am experiencing, but I now want to use 'thought language' to ask my own questions and receive my own answers about this relationship I am now exploring. *(Long pause of four or five minutes.)*

(Return to the present and awaken.)

Past-Life Involvement with My Present Mate or Lover Script

(Induction) "In this session I am going to go back in time to explore a lifetime, if one exists, in which (insert name) and I were together. If we have been together in more than one lifetime, the first time I do this session I'll perceive memories of the most important incarnation, in the following session the next most important lifetime, and so on. To communicate my desire to my subconscious mind, I will now concentrate on seeing the two of us together and mentally capturing both our essences. *(Pause for thirty seconds to imagine you and your mate/lover together. Call out your lover's name, silently, in your mind.)*

"All right, I am now going to go back in time to see if the two of us have indeed shared a previous incarnation. I will begin by stepping into the tunnel to my past and starting to move back in time. When I step out the other end of the tunnel, I will perceive impressions of the two of us together in another time and another place, if indeed this is reality." *(Complete the tunnel process.)*

"All right, I want to remember absolutely everything I am experiencing, but it is time to move on and explore a little more about this situation. Vivid impressions and new information now begin to flow into my mind." *(Pause.)*

(Again, try to identify the year and country, and if you're making a tape ask your own questions and receive your own answers. This means allowing the first situations you perceive to suggest the next questions, and so forth. Then, come back to the present and awaken.)

First Life on Earth Regression Script

(Induction) "In this session I am going to go way back in time to my very first earth lifetime. I will begin the experience by perceiving an important or clarifying situation that took place in my initial incarnation."

(Tunnel to the past, and pause to allow for initial impressions.) "All right, it is time to let go of this now, and to attain some additional information. First, I want to perceive the name of my people. I will trust and let the name come into my mind, if necessary one letter at a time." *(Pause.)*

"And I now want to become aware of what I do in this life I am now examining. How do I spend my time? Do I have any duties or any kind of job?" *(Pause.)*

"All right, I want to remember everything I am perceiving, but it is now time to explore how we are governed. When there is a group decision to be made, how is it determined?" *(Pause.)*

"And now, how do I get my food? When I am hungry, where do I go for food? Let vivid impressions begin to unfold." *(Pause.)*

"All right, it is time to use thought language to ask questions and receive the answers about this lifetime." *(Pause.)*

If you've scanned these scripts, you now have the understanding to begin writing your own. There is no end to the adventure.

CHAPTER

5

Parallel Lives

You are more than one person now living on the earth. Each one of them is a separate individual, yet each one is superconsciously connected to the other parallel selves who are influencing your current life.

This is one of the more difficult concepts for New Agers to accept and deal with. It really doesn't need to be, though, and it actually explains the apparent numerical problems presented by reincarnation.

Let's go back to the beginning of life on earth . . . and initially, please be aware that I am speaking symbolically. There was a time when there were no intelligent humans on the planet, but a great energy gestalt existed in the nonphysical realms. We'll call this gestalt "God," although any other name would do as well.

Now, we know from basic science that energy can't stand still. It must, by its very nature, create or destroy . . . it must expand or contract. So, as an expansion of the energy gestalt called God, the cells within the great body of God were constantly dividing and subdividing, always creating new energy, just as the cells within your physical body are always dividing and subdividing. This is a good analogy, for human beings are in fact made up of units of energy!

Let's call the new God cells "oversouls," each one part of the whole yet individual. And each oversoul would continue to expand the God energy by continuing to divide and subdivide. This is probably accomplished in many ways, with much of the process beyond our ability to comprehend. But let's explore how the oversouls might have implanted their essence as related to the three primary ways man came into being on the earth plane:

(1) As man evolved from ape to human, he eventually developed to the point where he could support intelligence, thus providing oversouls with another channel of expansion. The step from "animal" to "man" was made when the nonphysical oversouls began implanting their essence—their "soul atoms" —into physical human beings.

(2) As Edgar Cayce discussed in his readings, many experiments were conducted involving life on earth. The nonphysical oversouls explored direct manifestation from the spiritual to the physical planes. Once in a body of their own creation, their actions incurred karma and they were trapped on the physical plane, on the wheel of reincarnation, until the karmic debts could be resolved.

(3) As human history progressed, oversouls had further opportunity for the expansion of energy as beings from other planetary systems became involved in the evolution of our species. Humans whose genetic lineage includes extraterrestrial seeding retain deep subconscious memories of other star systems. Even today, some feel they do not belong here, without knowing why.

Eventually, the oversouls began to implant their soul atoms into more than one body at a time. This is why in the twentieth century, many oversouls are experiencing two or three physical incarnations at one time.

Stated another way, you may presently share a direct line of descent with one, two, or three other physical projections of your oversoul. This is the concept of "simultaneous multiple incarnations," which I call your "parallel selves." Unless parallel lives are a reality, reincarnation logically doesn't work, for the number of people living on this planet now is almost as large as the sum total of those that have ever lived here. So, there are not enough past lives to go around. I know that those doing the historical census are not including lost civilizations such as Lemuria and Atlantis, but that isn't really important. The many thousands of people I've regressed have experienced numerous past lives within recorded history as we know it. If they are representative of the rest of humanity, which seems logical, then numerically, reincarnation doesn't work.

So, if we accept the concept of parallels, there are really only a fraction as many people on earth as there appear to be. Take yourself as an example. You are yourself, but you may also have parallel selves— maybe a young boy in Vietnam . . . and an old woman in Mexico . . . and let's say, a middle-age doctor in London, England. You all share the same lineage, which is the past life lineage of your oversoul. You and your parallel selves are connected *superconsciously* . . . and you are influencing each other, although you don't realize this on a conscious level.

Let's explore this from a slightly different angle. Your oversoul exists on a nonphysical level and it explores a number of physical lifetimes as a way to multiply and expand its energy gestalt. In other words, at some point the cell we are calling your oversoul divided and you are one of the new ones that were created. You are one more in a long lineage of cells in the body of God—the part and whole at the same time. As an example: Any cell in your present, physical body contains your complete DNA—your genetic pattern or makeup. If humans could be cloned, as some reptiles can, you could be "duplicated" from that single cell.

In this situation, although your clone would only be part of your totality, from another perspective it would be your complete totality. Your oversoul was part of a lineage of cells or souls that leads directly back to the energy gestalt we called God. Thus, you are part of God—thus you are God. The part and the whole at the same time!

I first began to learn about parallel lives in 1974 while regressing a couple named Louise and Alex. The case history was included in You Were Born Again To Be Together (Pocket Books), which was published in April 1976. In the fall of 1976, Jane Roberts's book Psychic Politics came out. I didn't see Jane's manuscript and she didn't see mine. Yet this is what Seth had to say, channeling through Jane:

"Seth: If you could think of a multidimensional body existing at one time in different realities, and appearing differently within those realities, then you could get a glimpse of what is involved.

"You live more than one life at a time. You do not experience your century simply from one separate vantage point, and the individuals alive in any given century have far deeper connections than you realize. You do not experience your space-time world, then, from one but from many viewpoints."

In Past Lives, Future Loves (Pocket Books, 1978) I wrote of my own search for Ed Morrell, one of my parallel selves. A more complete version of the story was included as an epilogue to The Star Rover by Jack London (new edition 1983, Valley of the Sun Publishing). Also, Alan Weisman and Ruth Montgomery have written about the Morrell story in their books, although Ruth views the case as an example of a "walk-in." Walk-ins are entities who step into an adult body, by mutual agreement, if the residing soul desires to leave the earth plane because of "insurmountable circumstances." The walk-in bypasses the process of birth and childhood, retains the original owner's memories, and agrees to straighten out the usually messed-up life, as he proceeds with his own agenda.

You are God. Every living and discarnate individual is God. Together, we are an energy gestalt called God—an energy gestalt that continues to expand and procreate to produce more energy. God doesn't exist on a throne in heaven. He is you . . . and right now he is reading this book.

If you are hypnotically regressed to your most recent past life, you experience the life of your oversoul. If you are then regressed further, to the life before that one, you would be retracing your direct lineage and experiencing the life of your oversoul's oversoul.

The next important question is, "What happens to you at death?" Do you simply once more become part of the memory banks of your oversoul? *No— absolutely not. When you die, your knowledge and energy will remain throughout eternity as you.* And you are the sum total of all of the lives created by your direct lineage or frequency and the karmic heritage they have left.

Once anything is created, it is freed! You are an extension or creation of your oversoul and your oversoul has gained great awareness through your earth experience. You can call that awareness karma if you want to, for that is what it is. It is karma that you and your oversoul will continue to balance in the future.

Here is how the energy that is you continues to create and expand. After you experience physical death, you will cross over to the other side and find that you now have oversoul status. The way you will resolve your karma and engender additional energy is to continue the oversoul's process of division. In other words, you will implant your *soul atom* or essence into a new baby with a karmic configuration that supports your learning needs. Maybe you decide the best way to resolve your karma is to explore simultaneous lives as a businessman in Japan and a poor peasant in India. So, with the assistance of higher understanding, you implant your soul atom into two lives in those settings. And these two new human beings are extensions of yourself. Again, once anything is created, it is freed, so the two identities will not only be extensions of you but will also be free individuals. *They are on your "frequency" and you will feel and experience through them!* You will have to totally experience all their joys and misery, their successes and failures, *their learning! Which is your learning!* Thus you will continue to evolve through these additional lifetimes, raising your level of awareness.

Both of your extensions will share the same past-life lineage. In other words, if they were both hypnotically regressed, they would experience a past life as you, or as one of your present parallel selves. Or they could tap in on the earth life of your oversoul, or your oversoul's oversoul, and so forth, or any of the parallel beings in your direct oversoul lineage, all of whom would exist on the same frequency. Obviously, this means that each one of us could have far more past lives than traditional ideas about reincarnation would suggest.

The karma of your Japanese businessman and poor Indian peasant will be to master the lessons you didn't learn while you were on earth. Of course, they will also be the karmic beneficiaries of all the good karma you created during your physical life.

When these two extensions of you die, they will shape new channels for exploring their potential. Both will of course attain oversoul status upon their own crossover to the nonphysical realms. Thus the energy continues to multiply and expand.

If you examine the concepts I've discussed thus far, you'll find that they really negate little of the traditional perspective on how reincarnation and karma affect your life. It is still obvious that there is no way to escape your karmic responsibilities. Actually, this theory of reincarnation explains all the apparent fallacies I have encountered in my years of conducting past-life regressions. One is the numerical issue I've already mentioned. Another problem is one I have often experienced while working with extremely good regression subjects: I've found them living two lives within the same or overlapping historical time periods. Even more surprising, research has sometimes verified both existences and both lives appeared to be influencing the current lifetime.

Another example of the same phenomenon: A friend who is a regressive hypnotist once decided, if enough good subjects could be found, to explore the life of Christ through the observations of those who were actually there. By conducting some large group regressions he soon discovered several people who were able to relate vivid details about Jesus. None were key figures in the Passion, but they lived during the period and provided numerous facts and opinions about the Master. I felt that the odds of finding so many people with those memories were very small and that my friend was not being objective enough in his research. Yet, from the perspective I've just discussed, if the "cells" are continually doubling and tripling we would all soon have hundreds of thousands of past lives in our oversoul lineage. Then the probability of a "Jesus-link" might be much greater.

This concept of dividing cells of energy could also explain the Biblical statement that man was created in the image of God.

Any discussion of parallel selves in my seminars produces a flood of questions from the participants. Here are the ones most frequently asked:

Q: It sounds to me as though you're saying, "I've never actually been anyone else in a past life and I'll never be anyone else in a future life."

A: In fact, this may be the case, but you experience the effects almost exactly as they are presented in traditional reincarnational thinking. You are still the living result of all your past lives. Of course, the lives perceived by a psychic or explored through hypnotic regression are actually those of your oversoul lineage. But the lives are certainly affecting you today, just as if you yourself had actually lived them . . . which in a way you did.

Q: But you tell people they were born with a package of karma they wanted to experience. Obviously I didn't choose the karma . . . my oversoul did.

A: *No.* When the oversoul cell divides, it creates a new cell, a clone or duplicate of the original. You began your life as an exact duplicate of your oversoul. *Your* soul atom or cell was born with a background, a history, and with karma to experience. Your oversoul's desire was *your* desire, but once you were created, you were free. Thus, at the beginning of this life, you began to write your own script and create your own future. You initially drew upon the awareness and intuitive background of your oversoul creator, but with earthly experience comes true free choice.

Q: I can see that. But in the future, as an oversoul

myself, if I pass on my soul atom to others, it will be the others who experience the future life. I'm really off the hook . . . off the wheel of reincarnation!

A: Not really. What is the difference if you feel and experience through them? If you live completely all their joys and misery, their successes and failures, their learning? What's the difference if it's you or them? It amounts to a larger, maybe multidimensional you. Those whom you create to directly follow you will continue to work on your unfinished karma. The way you will evolve spiritually and raise your vibrational rate is to resolve disharmonious karma by letting go of fear and expressing unconditional love.

Nothing changes except your own awareness as to how the mechanics of reincarnation work. And by understanding the mechanics, you resolve the contradictions that always existed in the concept.

Q: Maybe you're right, but I'd prefer to continue to think of reincarnation as I always have in the past.

A: Do what works best for you. I can't see that either viewpoint would change anything in regard to how you walk a spiritual path.

Understanding your parallel selves can often help you to understand yourself, for you are all superconsciously connected and influencing each other. If your parallel is a farmer, you might have a gardening hobby. If your parallel plays the guitar, the instrument might be easier for you to learn. If your parallel has been injured in an accident, the connection might be experienced as depression. And as often as there are similarities, some parallel selves find that they are almost direct opposites—each learning a distinctively different aspect of life on earth.

During 1986, for the first time in nearly a decade, I included a parallel-life hypnotic transference session in several of my seminars *(see the script at the end of this chapter).* At the end of the sessions, the participants were asked to fill out a research sheet and describe their experiences. The following responses are typical of the hundreds of letters I received:

Fran Farmer, West Hollywood, CA: "The transference began in 1939, before I was born. All that I see is darkness and red. I have a great deal of pressure around my head, as if I am wearing a tight metal band around my crown. Then I begin to understand that I am a Tibetan lama who has lived for a very long time in a building that is old and solid, but dark. I am a monk involved in philosophic studies. The high point in my life was meeting the Dalai Lama. I had a private audience with him in which he presented me with the red scarf of protection and honor. He laid it across my outstretched hands which I held in a prayer position as I knelt before him. Then we sat on our cushions and we ate and conversed. It was a very relaxed and joyous day for me. After the meal we walked toward one of the tall, thin windows of the temple and gazed out at the country below.

"When you asked about hobbies, I was confused. I'm not sure if this is because I do not differentiate between studies and hobbies, or if I simply have little time for them. However, I receive a special joy from art, herbology, and astrology. At the end, when you asked, "How could you communicate with your parallel?" the me here in this seminar realized that we already know how and are in communication—astrally."

Gundela McCabe, West Covina, CA: "I tapped in on my parallel self back in 1946. At that time she was a woman approximately forty years old. Her name is Nurmi Kindahar, and she is the wife of a well-to-do merchant, Kandar. She does not work, and her hobby is the embroidery of richly colored red and blue saris with gold threads. She lives in New Delhi, India, in what looks like an apartment building. They occupy the penthouse and have no children. The most important event in her life was to hear Indira Ghandi speak about freedom. Ever since, she has secretly worked for the freedom movement, although her husband does not appreciate this.

"In my current life I have no special feelings for India, however I do feel very involved with freedom movements for anything—not just ERA or such, but freedom for everyone from everything."

Nancie Lesko, Morrison, CO: "I saw a young boy in 1973 carrying a machine gun. There was much sadness in his eyes. Guatemala was the country, but they lived in tent cities because they were always on the move. He felt very close to his mother and took care of her and her four children. His name was Juan Tephu. I could feel that he felt the weight of the world on his shoulders, always having to be grown up. The only escape he had was swimming and diving. Maybe that could explain why sometimes I feel like crying for absolutely no reason, the tears just springing to my eyes! Also, my favorite thing is swimming in the ocean, diving, and snorkeling."

Beth Carr Sorensen, Littleton, CO: "I should preface this by saying that I have always avoided discussions with my husband about being a housewife and raising children. I've driven myself to obtain an education, find work, and start down a career path.

"My parallel self is a housewife in Illinois. I saw her in 1968 and know her name is Betty Beales. Her husband is named Jerry. She's in her mid-thirties and is everything that I've always rebelled against being. She keeps house, has children, and has a best friend named Cara who she confides in and trusts more than her husband. She appears to be politically unaware, even uncaring—she doesn't follow current events at all. I have enough other information about her to make an attempt to locate her. I think it's funny that my ego-self wanted my parallel to have an exotic, exciting life, and it turned out to be a life that I've always said I'd never have!"

Audrey Cosenza, Hollywood, CA: "I saw a Vietnamese or Filipino man in his mid-forties working on a potter's wheel in a white building. Similarities: I work in clay and have always been fascinated by it, even as a child. In the altered state, as I watched this man making a vase, I thought to myself, 'Oh, so that's how you do it.' It was as though he were teaching me."

Patti Cunningham, Ft. Lauderdale, FL: "I saw a small village at the foot of a mountain, and a beautiful Oriental house and garden. I am also an Oriental lady, born April 4, 1956. The lady is very petite, but her face is misty, unclear. Her family is the most important thing to her and she lives a very domestic life-style, uninvolved with money or business. She spends some of her time gardening. Her grandmother is also very important to her.

"My parallel seems to have all the things in her life I do not. I am far away from my family, have no children, am divorced, self-supporting, work a full-time job, and have to deal with money and business for survival. She is taken care of and gives nuturing in return; I am self-sufficient and have worked in psychiatric nursing, putting the focus on helping people learn responsibility and independence. She has stable relationships; I do not. I have at times longed for a domestic life-style. She has at times wanted to be involved in the world outside the home."

Parallel Self-Transference Session Script

(Do the induction first.) "And I am now completely relaxed and at ease and ready to explore a tie between myself and one of my parallel selves, if indeed this

concept is valid and these other aspects of my totality have existed between my birth and this moment. I realize a parallel self could have died or could have just been born somewhere else in the world. There are as many possibilities as there are people who have been alive while I have been living my current life.

"If indeed I am experiencing other explorations of my oversoul's potential, in other bodies, my own superconscious mind is fully aware of this fact. My Higher Self knows anything and everything that relates to me, and since it is part of the collective unconscious, it can draw from all knowledge throughout all of time.

"And I am now going to seek to establish a tie with a parallel self. I have the power and ability to allow a mental transference to take place and to perceive my parallel life only as an observer, without pain or emotion. And I am now going to count backward from seven to one, and on the count of one, the transference will be complete and I will perceive impressions of my parallel. If I have more than one parallel, I will leave it up to my Higher Self to direct me to the identity which will best serve my awareness at this time.

"And I am now letting go and beginning to transcend time and space. Moving through time and space . . . activating a transference . . . *(count very slowly or insert dialogue between the counts)* number seven . . . number six . . . number five . . . number four . . . number three . . . number two . . . and on the next count, I will perceive my parallel self and explore an aspect of my parallel's life . . . number one.

(If necessary to begin the impressions use the same techniques you used in past-life regression—"Am I outdoors or indoors?" "What is my parallel wearing on

his feet?" etc. Pause long enough to observe every detail of your initial impressions.)

"Note the year—if necessary, one number at a time. *(Pause.)* What is the city and country I find myself experiencing? *(Pause.)* What does my parallel do for a living? *(Pause.)* What are my parallel's hobbies or special interests? *(Pause.)* Which other person is most important to my parallel? *(Pause.)* And I am now going to move backward or forward in time to a very important event in my parallel's life. On the count of three, I'll be there and vivid impressions will begin to come in. One, two, three. *(Pause.)* What is my parallel's name, one letter at a time? *(Pause.)* How could I contact my parallel directly, person to person? *(Pause. If you desire, leave additional time to ask your own questions.)*

"All right, it's now time to let go of this and return to the present in my own life. I will awaken, remembering everything I have just experienced about my parallel life, and if I consciously desire, I can now draw more knowledge and awareness than ever before from my parallel self." *(Awaken script.)*

CHAPTER

6

Automatic Writing

Susan A. Matuszak, West Springfield, MA: "I was first exposed to automatic writing at your Sedona Psychic Seminar in October, 1985. At the time, I didn't believe that I could do it. I was astounded when the pen began flying across the paper, revealing information of value. I have since used the technique often and have taught it to many people in the Connecticut area.

"Attached is a sample of what I received. I have underlined two particular passages I found to be very interesting as well as inspirational.

7/1/87 (seeking information on love): *Oh, my dear child, you have come so far . . . and you have so far to go. But keep that smile on your face. For every day is a creation and every day is a time to celebrate existence in God's world. Take the time you need to learn the truth for <u>it is in truth we gain wisdom and in wisdom we gain God</u>. Love, love, and love. As you are learning, it is not always being nice that creates the right way for the right situation. It is in love that we allow others to grow and also gain wisdom.*

"*Do not fear the unknown. The nations are ever*

friendly. What you have to do is step closer to the truth. Be quiet when you walk, but be loud in your actions. Learn to trust your guardians . . . as we never leave you. We are here.

"Let the flame of love grow brightly every day. It is to be seen and used. It is to be. It is your path. It won't be easy, but it will be a giant leap into God. For you realize that it has to be.

"Don't fear. There are many by your side helping you, assisting you along the way. Create the space for them; thus, you create your reality. Learn to see the masses for what they are and play the role you have been assigned.

"Look to each obstacle as a learning experience and it will no longer become an emotional toil for you to endure it. Leave behind what is not important and move to the next step. Create the reality as honestly as you can, knowing that honesty will see you through.

"Feed the flame of hope into the eyes of the masses. Let them know of thy care and that they are cared for. <u>Let your eyes shine as never before, as your light is much more than a flicker, it is a fire of love and light. Remember it is made by God. Yes, as you are God.</u> We so love you and the work you are doing.

"Pick up the paint brush and create the colors of love. Create the story as it was never told before. Create to express the eternal."

"Who are you?" Susan asked mentally.

"I am one of many painting the colors of your life. We are the paint and you are the canvas. Allow us to occasionally dip the paint brush and do our work along thy path also, as we have assignments, too, you know. I am Sir Mandell and was a 17th-century painter. We are many here. I just speak at this time to bring to you the awareness of the power and beauty of your paint."

"Thank you, Sir Mandell. May we meet again?" Susan asked.

"We have never parted. With much love and respect, Sir Mandell."

Kym Caraway, Phoenix, AZ: "In 1973, a Texas psychic told me one of my guides was a doctor and that he wanted to contact me through automatic writing. On my first attempt, I got *'Help me, please help me!'* I was fearful to begin with and that did it. I called the psychic and he told me never to do it without a prayer of protection.

"On the next attempt, the pencil started to fly across the page, line after line of handwriting totally unlike mine. In summary, it said, *"Sarah has waited so long to be with you and it's time you let her through!"* I had tried for years to get pregnant using every technique available, including fertility drugs. Nothing worked and I gave it up. Another pertinent fact: I was married to an alcoholic.

"The automatic writing went on to say the reason I hadn't conceived was that I subconsciously feared my child having an alcoholic father. I grew up with an alcoholic father. The writing said this was not my decision to make. I was told to start changing my mind-set by telling people I would get pregnant, would have a little girl and her name would be Sarah.

"I followed the instructions, although many friends —as well as my born-again Christian family— thought I'd gone off the deep end and wanted me to find professional help. Three months later, my pregnancy was confirmed. I decided to name the child Sara if it was a girl (dropping the h). The next automatic writing said, *'We have to tell you Sarah wants her name to be spelled with an h at the end. She also says to tell you that she will wait long enough to be okay, but not as long as you think to be born. She has waited so long, she will wait just long enough.'*

"Sarah was born premature, jaundiced, and had to remain in the hospital awhile. I left her father when she was three months old. When I eventually had a numerology chart done for Sarah, I was told that souls impress the desired name into the minds of the parents-to-be to assure the proper vibrational rate. The numerologist became excited and showed me how that 'h' was of the utmost importance to my baby's name. Her astrology is almost totally outgoing, with hardly any introverted tendencies. It says that she will most likely be very career-oriented, in the public eye, and potentially unbalanced in that there's very little reservation. The spelling of Sarah with the 'h' brings a degree of balance to her chart."

Lori L. Dingman, Perry, MI: "One day, while I was involved in my normal activities, an internal voice said, *'Within the hearts of all men burns the flame of the Christ spirit.'* I thought, 'That's very poetic.' (I'm not a poet.) I got a pen and paper and wrote it down. No sooner had I written it down than my hand took off and started writing. The words came so fast, I could barely keep up with the dictation. Since then, I have taken to using the typewriter during my automatic writing sessions. It is the only way I can keep up. Enclosed are some samples of messages I've received. I can stop the dictation at any time with a question, or to discuss anything that is on my mind."

7/11/87: *"Typing is very good. It is much faster. As we learn the keyboard, it will become the most efficient way to communicate. You can take care of the spelling and we will dictate."*

Lori: "Who is Minjh?"

"Minjh is or was a person you knew in a past life, in India in the fourth millennium. You do not have recall of that life as you do of others. There were many great tribes in India at that time. You were a woman and Minjh was your husband; he is now the person you know as your uncle. Your debt to him was balanced long ago. The purpose for your association in this life is

to help him to understand himself, though it is a minor association in this life. Your main relationship is with your husband. This is your perfect outworking with your husband. There is much good in the relationship and much more good can come if you both will work at it. Be kind to one another. This is the best advice we can give you."

Lori: "Where have I known my mother before?"

"You have known your mother in many lifetimes. The last time you were together, you were the mother and she was the daughter. Much of that relationship has carried over from a seventh-century lifetime in Greece."

Lori: "Was I in Pompeii?"

"Yes, you were there, though you made your home in a small fishing village. It was a very happy, contented life. You have lived many lifetimes, as has each individual on the earth, trying to learn his lessons in order to progress. We will tell you about those lifetimes at another time. You are getting tired. Be at peace. The Masters of the Seven Rays."

7/21/87: *"Hello. We welcome all of mankind to our consciousness, for we are the consciousness of love, joy, and peace. Meditate on these things and learn to express them more fully."*

Lori: "What is your message for today?"

"Today we wish to talk about the nature of man's free will. Free will was given by the creator so that man would be able to express love to his fullest potential. This is a double-edged blade, however. As well as having free expression, man also has the potential to abuse it. When fear entered human consciousness, free will turned from a loving, joyful expression to one of ignorance and doubt. The expression of free will produced all the lower emotions. Man saw himself as separate from God and separate from all his brothers and sisters. This was the fall from grace, the figurative

'eating of the forbidden fruit.' Yes, it was a sad thing, but there was still hope, still time to return to the true self.

"It saddens us greatly to see all that goes on every day on the beautiful jewel known as earth. There is so much negativity that it looks to us like a dense black fog penetrating everything on the planet.

"Now is the time of mankind's awakening, however, and a few lights are beginning to penetrate the dense fog. This is why you must unite with others of like minds and hearts. Together, you can break up the negativity. Think on these things. Meditate on them, and unite as brothers and sisters of the light. Herald the New Age by remembering your true self, your God-self. There is no separation from God. There never has been. Be at peace, we are with you always and we are the Masters of the Seven Rays."

Marion Former, Lowell, MA: "In 1984, I read <u>A Search for Truth</u> by Ruth Montgomery. She offered instructions on how to do automatic writing. My first attempt was an illegible scrawl, but I could read the word 'Moon' in several of the lines. With a couple of days' practice, the writing had improved sufficiently for me to be able to read at least half of what was written. I discovered that Moon was my spirit guide. In fact, he called himself my 'soulmate.' According to him, the bond of love had always existed between us since before the creation of the physical universe. He was watching over me and waiting impatiently for me to return to what he termed 'true reality.'

"After a couple of weeks of this I thought I must have some kind of mental disorder. Yet, at the same time, it totally fascinated me and I began to look forward to the writing sessions. I also began meditating each day.

"By this time, I was hearing the words in my head even as my hand was writing them. I purchased a home computer and since then have typed the messages and saved them on disks. As you can imagine, I now have a tremendous amount of information on many varied subjects.

"My doubts about my mental stability continued until I had a reading with a psychic. She uses psychometry and automatic writing. I was asked to write one question on a piece of paper and keep the paper with me during the reading, but I was not to show it to her or tell her what the question was. I decided to ask, 'Who is Moon?' because I was really curious to find out whether my experience was coming from outside of myself. The psychic knew nothing of what had been happening to me. At the end of the reading, she channeled the following message for me in answer to my written question:

> *Swept by the waves of the ocean,*
> *Down through the winds of time,*
> *I watch you with sweet remembrance,*
> *You are mine, dear love, all mine.*

The psychic told me that, while she was writing, she had felt the presence of a very strong force, a soul who was very different from those whom she usually encountered while receiving messages. The feeling reminded her of a dark entity who had pursued Taylor Caldwell through many of her previous lives. This information was given in the book, <u>The Search for a Soul</u>, by Jess Stearn. She told me to try to find the book and read it, which I did. I could see why she felt the similarity. Right from the beginning Moon had written that he was a dark soul who had found the light but could fall again.

"From that point on I began to accept what I was channeling without too much thought about how genuine it was. Moon predicted the space-shuttle disaster five months before it happened. He supplied pertinent past-life readings for people I know nothing about, their names given to me by friends and family. Many of his writings reflect the dual nature of everything, the light and the dark. He constantly stresses how all souls are eternal, with choice and free will.

"Moon has said he talks to me in dreams of which I have no memory, but I often experience what I call 'flashes' which, according to him, are recalled memories of what he told me while I slept. I usually feel very peaceful and relaxed when I channel and this calmness stays with me for some time after a session is over. Like most people, my life is often hectic, frustrating, and sometimes very unhappy, but I now have an inner sense of peace that his teachings have brought to me. I believe there are no accidents—we do create our own reality. We perpetuate this self-created reality by choosing the people and the circumstances we experience.

"I am enclosing some messages Moon has written about himself at different times:

9/3/84: (In response to the question 'Who are you?') *"Mighty warrior, prince, cherished one, fallen one, Lord of all Pleteris. I am Moon, Thebeus, Cantor Soccho, Danus, Melpher, and many more. I am an archangel, a wizard, a poet, a warrior, a deceiver, a fulfiller, a dark soul that has found salvation."*

5/12/85: *"Come forth and read my words, all those who doubt that I am Moon. I am the one I say I am and I have seen and done the things of which I tell. I have watched worlds be born, and others die. I have marched with armies through desolate wastes, spurred on by the desire to kill for glory. I have crossed the vastness of space and viewed a million galaxies. I have looked upon the abyss and know that there lies true evil, for it contains no form or pattern.*

"I have climbed the mountains of Ixa, Gomothe, and

*Earth, and I have swum in their bright rivers, too. I
know the pain and sorrow of the flesh and I am here to
tell you that they are but transient things for the endless
soul to ponder upon. I have dwelt within a tiny flower
and felt its joy when the rain washed and nourished it,
and I have been one with the fiery particles of a comet
as it blazed across the skies of many worlds. I have been
arrogant, treacherous, and destructive, yet I strive for
the true wisdom of love. I write of the oneness that was
and will be again, though different, for in true reality
the oneness is and has never ceased. Do not doubt me, I
exist even as you do."*

Automatic writing is one of my favorite techniques
to teach in a seminar because almost every participant
will quickly experience results. Ideally, I spend half a
day teaching it, first talking about the subject and
relating my own experiences as well as those of author
friends. Then, after giving exact instructions, I induce
group hypnosis and direct a powerful automatic writing session, giving the participants twenty minutes of
quiet time to receive the writing. For the next session,
I instruct them to find a partner, someone they did not
know before the beginning of the seminar. Next, they
go into an altered state on their own and use automatic writing to do a psychic reading on their partner.
The success rate is phenomenal, and skeptics are often
converted on the spot.

Just about anyone interested in metaphysics is
aware of the many books Ruth Montgomery has
written using automatic writing. Each morning, she
sits down at her electric typewriter, says a prayer, and
allows Lily and the group to communicate through
her hands. One morning, nearly twelve years ago,
shortly before my son Travis was born, Ruth received
some writing about him and why he was coming into

this incarnation. She sent it to me, but it was somehow lost in the mail.

It was a few months after Travis was born that I first learned of the writing. Ruth and I were working together at a Phoenix, Arizona, seminar. I think it was because I was so upset about not receiving the information that the following morning Ruth asked her guides for the information once again, this time by hand. At breakfast, she handed me this page of writing:

Nov. 11—Phoenix: (symbol) Lily—Travis is a highly developed entity who chose his parents for the outstanding work they will be doing in making preparations for the New Age. He is a remarkable soul who reached a high level of development in a life in Turkey in the fifteenth century, bringing enlightenment to that warlike area and leading many along the path that broke through the barriers of the Dark Ages. His mission now is to lead others out of the chaos following the axis shift and into the New Age of enlightenment. This is a good area in which to pursue that endeavor and he will advance rapidly, for his parents will release him from restraints and let his free will soar. He will be a leader among men, as he has been many times before. All for now—Love from us here.

Jess Stearn introduced me to my wife and is one of our closest friends. He lives just down the road from us in Malibu and we often get together for dinner and weekend gatherings. In 1985, I produced a series of tapes called Ask the Experts for Valley of the Sun Publishing. The tapes are made up of interviews with many friends in the New Age field. Jess was part of the project, as were Brad Steiger, Steven Halpern, Charles

Thomas Cayce, Dr. Edith Fiore, Alan Vaughan, and others.

One of the subjects was channeling (verbally or via automatic writing). This is some of what Jess had to say:

"Arthur Ford, the great medium, was an intimate friend of mine. He visited me in my home and I visited him down in Florida. I loved him dearly. Toward the end of his career, we were talking about the authenticity of his communications. He said, 'You know, Jess, at this point in my life, I sometimes question myself. I even question Fletcher, my guide whom I believe in so implicitly. I wonder if I was just dramatizing my own subconscious.'

"I responded by saying 'Arthur, it really doesn't make much difference, does it? You don't know where the information is coming from, you haven't misrepresented anything. Maybe the information is coming from an experience you had before, or from a past life, or from the Universal intelligence. What difference does a name make? The only thing that really matters is the truth of whatever it is that came through you.'"

Dick: "Jess, are you willing to talk about the contacts you had with Edgar Cayce while you were writing the book about him?"

"Yes. In the early '60s, I was writing and researching my book, <u>A Door to the Future</u>. I went to Virginia Beach to visit the A.R.E. (Association For Research And Enlightenment). The reception from the A.R.E. people was overwhelming. I'd been working for big-city newspapers and <u>Newsweek</u>, but I'd never received a reception like this. They opened everything up to me. Hugh Lynn Cayce even gave me a key to the library so I could do research at 2 A.M. if I wanted to.

"A day or so after I arrived, Hugh Lynn said, 'I have something I want to show you. It might surprise you.' It was a reading by Edgar Cayce done in 1931 when I was still a kid. It said, 'Be good to Stearn when he comes down from New York because he will be of great value to the organization.'

"So, I looked up at Hugh Lynn and said, 'Well, there are a lot of Stearns in New York, how do I know it's me?' So he showed me another one. Cayce did all these readings about what he called 'the work.' The third reading caused my stomach to kick over because it said, 'Have Dave Conn tell Stearn about the work.' Conn was the guy in New York who first mentioned Edgar Cayce to me five years earlier in Harold Riley's office when he found out I was interested in the esoteric. Nobody knew about that.

"One evening, after A Door to the Future was published, I was having dinner with the president of Doubleday, my publishing company. He asked, 'What's your next book?' I explained I was working on a book about 'the psychic age' but I didn't seem to be getting anywhere with it. He said, 'Why don't you write about Edgar Cayce? I think everyone would be interested in that.'

"Back in my apartment, late at night, I decided to act on his suggestion. I was going through my files on Cayce when the phone rang. It was a medium I knew, a Madam Basheeba. She had gained some notoriety by telling the mayor of Chicago to be very careful with whom he sat in public. Somebody was going to take a shot at a man more prominent than he. If he wasn't careful, the bullet might hit him. He laughed and told the newspaper people about it. Sometime later he was sitting with Roosevelt, shortly after the president's inauguration, in Florida when an assassin shot at Roosevelt. The bullet was deflected and killed the mayor. The papers reported the story and made Madam Basheeba quite famous. At any rate, I was expected to listen to her.

"She called me shortly before 1 A.M. and said, 'Jess,

Edgar Cayce just came to me. We had a long conversation. He is very pleased that you're going to be doing this book about him.'

"At this time I'd told no one, having just decided to do the book.

"Basheeba continued, 'Yes, he's very pleased. He wants you to know that, and he wants to help you.'

"'How's he going to help me?' I asked.

"'Well, he has a title for the book. It's to be called <u>The Sleeping Prophet.</u>'

"So I wrote all this down and then she told me, 'He wants you to get into reincarnation. He wants you to talk about Dr. Ketchum. He wants you to talk about the life readings and prophecies and predictions. If you do all that, you'll write the book very easily and it will become the number one best-seller in the country.'

"So I accepted what she told me, because there was no harm in accepting it. She also said, 'Anytime you run into any difficulty, he'll look over your shoulder and be ready to help you.'

"Well, Dick, it took me only three weeks to write that book. One chapter was troublesome, so I asked, 'Edgar, help me out.' I don't want to borrow any of Ruth Montgomery's concepts, but I honestly think he *walked in.* I felt his presence very strongly and suddenly saw the subject of the chapter in a different light. It made it very easy for me to finish the book."

Brad Steiger has written over one hundred metaphysical books since 1956, a record unmatched by anyone else in the field. We had just completed a national seminar tour together and were both living in Scottsdale, Arizona, in 1978 when Brad decided to write his first novel. After so many nonfiction books, this was a major transition and he was understandably a little nervous about it.

At lunch one day, I asked him how it was coming.

"Well, I've decided to get a little help," he responded, and asked that I keep this confidential. "I decided to ask for the assistance of the two writers I most admire, Nathaniel Hawthorne and Edgar Allan Poe. With their help, it's going very well."

The book was called The Hypnotist. Shortly after Brad submitted the final manuscript to his agent, the agent called and said, "Brad, I love the book, but it's weird! It reads like Hawthorne, Poe, and you!"

Once the book was published, Brad no longer minded if the story was told. I never asked him exactly what techniques he employed to get the extra help, but I do recall hearing him say, "I'm using my little rituals!"

The Donning International Encyclopedic Psychic Dictionary by June G. Bletzer defines automatic writing:

> *To allow an etheric world intelligence to intervene in one's hand and arm and write on paper information that one had no way of knowing from formal education or life experiences; medium must have the proper body chemistry, know how to relax and keep the conscious mind neutral; medium holds pen in hand over the paper until the intelligence enters and moves the hand and pen/ pencil; writing is swift, and frequently runs together as if the entity would lose control if he or she picked the pen up from word to word; writing could be large and slanting; accomplished in trance state or an awareness state appearing that the medium was entirely conscious.*

I would agree with everything but the part about "body chemistry." I've found that anyone can learn to do automatic writing if they are properly instructed, enter an altered state of consciousness, and are willing to work at it. Body chemistry might, however, explain some of the cases of accidental automatic writing. In <u>You Were Born Again to Be Together</u> (Pocket Books 1976), I told a story about my sister-in-law. She was sitting at the kitchen table, having her morning coffee and doodling with a pencil, when her hand began to write on its own. Large writing asked that she change hands. She is left-handed, but when the pencil was transferred to her right hand, the entity responsible for the transmissions explained that he had been right-handed while living on the earth.

Lillian Bateman of Abbotsford, B.C., Canada sent me an account of an "uninvited episode of automatic writing I was afflicted with in 1962." Today, she is seventy-four and is still looking for answers as to why she had the experiences. "Does heredity have anything to do with it?" she asked. "My great grandmother was a Highland Scot reputed to have 'second-sight!'"

Lillian was a registered nurse when the writing began. "I had perched on my usual stool in front of the desk by the window, idly wondering what I'd need to order for nursery supplies. Traffic flowed by on the street below, my pen was poised above the slip of paper as I mentally counted out the cans of Similac left on the shelf in the milk lab, when my right arm started to tingle, and the hairs on it began to rise. I thought for a second that I'd unknowingly bumped my 'funny-bone' . . . only I knew I hadn't.

"While I ran through all the explanations I could think of, my hand cramped, my fingers grasped the pen, and it began to move independently of my will, leaving queer tracks that I suppose could be called writing. My first thought was, 'My God! I'm having a stroke!' and I jumped up, dropping the pen, and stood there stupidly rubbing the affected arm. It felt perfectly normal now, my fingers worked, there was no more of the tingling sensation. If not a stroke, perhaps a sort of cerebral spasm, and in that case I'd better check my eyes. Going to a mirror over the sink in the formula room, I stared at my pupils. Both were equal in size, although perhaps a bit dilated. That was all. Other reflexes tested normal as well. A check of my blood pressure proved it was normal.

"Returning to the desk, I wondered if it had all been a product of my imagination and I returned to the task of ordering the supplies. Upon retrieving the fallen pen, I grasped it firmly and wrote briskly. Done! I had no interference until I paused to concentrate on other supplies. As soon as I relaxed my grip, the pen, the tingly arm, and the whole silly business began all over again. This time, I didn't panic. I made myself relax and watch.

"At first, the pen made spirals and scrolls, but it soon developed a rhythm and uniformity of line. Fascinated, I saw it draw a neat circle and from this develop an entire flower—petals, leaves, and stem—without lifting from the paper or retracing a single line. (Later I learned it would never lift from the paper during the process.) Halfway down the page, something like a script developed—neat, straight across the page—something with a pattern to it, but unreadable. It almost appeared to be backward writing. Feeling very foolish, I took the paper to the mirror and read, 'message for mary . . . agnes.' There were no capitals or punctuation.

"At lunch I asked Mary, a nurse's aide, 'Do you know anyone called Agnes?' Mary stopped as if I'd struck her, stared at me, then burst into tears.

"'What a mean thing for you to say to me!' Mary responded. 'You must know I was a friend of Agnes. Don't you remember the woman who died just four months ago? Well, that was Agnes!' Before I could apologize, she ran off down the hall, sobbing."

Lillian explained how the writing soon became a part of her life. Her contacts called themselves "Phyrros," and were soon providing reams of information about the esoteric world. "I didn't appreciate my new gift," she said. "It upset my routine. I was curious and wasted my spare time with the writing. I asked how these transmissions were sent and was told they used the hemoglobin in the bloodstream."

In an attempt to close down the automatic writing, Lillian asked to be checked out by some people with the local Edgar Cayce group. "Professor Ballbrush in Los Angeles said I was a natural medium. I wanted no part of it, so he said he'd help me close my chakras. Two twenty-minute sessions and my problems were over. The writing ceased, the hand cramps that had plagued me to write when I didn't want to, ceased, and I was free to be myself again."

HOW TO DO AUTOMATIC WRITING

Use automatic writing only if and when you want to do it. Never under any conditions allow the unseen to dictate to you. A wise entity will gently guide but will never tell you exactly what to do. Be wary; stop writing if you should receive such advice or vile language.

First, pick a time and place where it is perfectly quiet and you will not be interrupted. A semi-dark room is ideal. Use a large writing or drawing pad and a smooth-writing pen; felt-tipped pens seem to work the best. Then do at least ten minutes of deep yoga breathing (described in the last chapter of this book in conjunction with "the induction"). While you sit comfortably with the pad in your lap, swirl overlapping ovals across the page with your pen. Hold the pen loosely in your hand and keep your wrist like a rubber band, loose and relaxed. Practice closing your eyes while continuing the spirals. Open them but not all the way. Don't focus on the page; unfocus your eyes, or focus beyond the page. This ten-minute period is to relax your body and to quiet your mind. When outside thoughts come in, simply brush them aside and think only of the blank page before you.

Next, when you are very relaxed and your mind is quiet, begin "the induction." I'd suggest that you make a tape of it followed by the "Automatic Writing Script" at the end of these instructions. That way all you have to do is click on the player. The tape then assists you to establish white light protection and will guide you into the writing process without your having to consciously think about it.

From this point on the process is self-explanatory, but here is a tip that may be of value: Once you hear the instructions telling you to allow the information to come through, just barely open your eyes (this will not awaken you) and begin the swirls. Never let your pen stop. If it takes off on its own, get out of the way—mentally and physically—and let it happen. The automatic writing has begun. Don't attempt to read and understand the writing as it is coming through. This can pull your conscious mind back into the process and the cycle-per-second activity of your brain could move back up into a beta level.

Another tip: If, after swirling for a while, the automatic writing hasn't begun to flow but you are receiving strong thoughts about something, go ahead and write down your thoughts. Use the same loose motion you've used with the swirls. You are initially writing your thoughts with the full awareness of what you are doing, but very often the pen will just take off on its own. It may take several practice sessions to get the "feel" of automatic writing, but it will work.

Automatic writing usually works best if you have a specific question in mind. I always suggest that you write the question at the top of the page. You will be open to receiving information only from your own Higher Self, your guides, Masters, highly evolved or loving entities who mean you well, or from those whom you request contact with, such as a deceased relative or wise soul. At first, until you have become proficient with the technique, you may not want to limit the information you can receive by specifying who is to supply it. In other words, if your guide knows the answer and is available to communicate it to you, you might learn more from him than by calling on your deceased grandmother.

Automatic Writing Script

(Induction first) "And I am now relaxed and at ease and peacefully centered. I feel in balance and in harmony. A quietness of spirit permeates my body and mind, as I now open to become a channel for successful automatic writing. I absolutely have the power and ability to step outside myself and allow the energy of my Higher mind, or an entity of my choice, to communicate with me through my hand, via automatic writing.

"And I now focus upon what I desire to learn through automatic writing. I simplify my question to one well-worded sentence, which I will now repeat over and over as a mental mantra. I will also meditate upon the source of the information I wish to access."

(Allow at least one minute of silence for this.)

"And it is now time to call in my guides and Masters to assist me to intensify the connection and to spiritually protect me during this session."

(Call out silently in your mind to them. Hear your voice echo across the Universe, then return to you. Allow at least forty-five seconds for this.)

"And it is now time to intensify the spiritual protection, so I begin to visualize very, very vividly, a bright white light coming down from above and entering the crown chakra of spirituality on the top of my head. This is the Universal light of life energy . . . the God light. See it! Feel it! A shimmering, iridescent beam of bright white light, entering my crown chakra and beginning to flow through my body and mind. I feel it flowing through me and beginning to concentrate around my heart area. And I now imagine the light emerging from my heart area and totally surrounding me with an aura of protection. *(Pause.)* And I seek Divine protection in the white light of God's love. I seek protection from all things seen and unseen, all forces and all elements. Protect me throughout this session, assuring only sincere contact with highly evolved and loving entities, or with Higher Mind. And protect me through the days, weeks, months and years that follow. I ask it, I beseech it, I mark it, and so it is. *(Pause.)* And I am totally protected. Only my own guides and Masters, or those I invite, may communicate through my hand.

"And now, it is time to connect with the source of the information I seek to come through my hand. I do this now. I imagine the source and silently in my mind make my wishes known."

(Allow at least forty seconds to make this connection. Imagine it vividly.)

"All right, in just a moment I will open my eyes and begin writing. I absolutely have the power and ability to allow the energy to flow through me and to receive awareness through this technique. When I open my eyes, they will be just barely open, and I will keep my pen moving at all times. On the count of three, I will open my eyes and begin to write automatically. Number one, number two, number three."

(Take as long as you want to do the writing. At the end of the session you can awaken yourself with the following, or, if you're using a tape, you can record the awakening at the end.)

"The writing is now complete and it is time to return. So I close my eyes and take a few moments to thank the source of my information. *(Pause for at least ten seconds to thank your source.)* And it is now time to return to full beta consciousness. On the count of five I will open my eyes and be wide awake, remembering everything I just experienced in the session. I will awaken fully alert, thinking and acting with calm self-assurance . . . feeling glad to be alive and at peace with myself, the world and everyone in it. *(Count up from one to five.)*"

CHAPTER

7

Psychometry

Glen Anthony Young, Kansas City, MO: "While seeing a psychic for a reading in April of 1988, she told me, 'I believe you have a natural gift for psychometry.' She then took off her watch and handed it to me. I had never attempted psychometry before, but I had read quite a bit about it. I took the watch in both hands. Closing my eyes, I breathed deeply and relaxed as best I could, but all I received was a physical sensation of tingling with some pain behind my knees and in my thighs. I attributed this to nervousness.

"I waited for something more to come, but nothing did. What I'd experienced seemed unimportant, but since I had nothing else to report, I told the woman about it. She asked me if the feeling was stronger in one of the legs. 'No, it was equal in both my legs,' I replied. She then explained that she had arthritis flare-ups in the exact locations I described, affecting both legs equally. It was obvious to her that I had picked up her pain, which had been acute in the week preceding my reading.

Patricia Rardin, Corning, CA: "One day while talking about metaphysics with a friend, she handed me her wedding ring and asked me to do psychometry. I told her that I had never done it, but she insisted that I try. Holding the ring, I immediately began to receive mental pictures. I saw her standing with her husband in what appeared to be an office and described the room in detail. There was another man in a dark blue business suit, speaking to them. I couldn't hear the conversation, but I knew that he was telling them something good—something that would give them some relief from tension.

"Two weeks later, my friend called me to say that half of what I told her had happened. She and her husband had gone to a nearby town to see a specialist their family physician had arranged for them to see. The doctor fit my physical description exactly, but he was wearing a white medical jacket and tan slacks. She said that the furniture in the room was identical to my description, but the shape of the room and the wall color were not right. Instead of telling them something good, the specialist told her husband that he needed immediate surgery.

"At the end of the week, I received another call from my friend. She told me that she was sitting in the hospital waiting room just off the surgery section waiting for her husband's operation to be completed. As she looked around, she realized that the shape of the room and color of the walls were exactly as I had described in my reading. Later, when the doctor came in to talk to her, he was wearing a dark blue business suit, just as I had mentioned in the reading. He told her that her husband had done very well in surgery and should be completely recovered within a few weeks.

"What was fascinating to me about this was that I had integrated two separate events into one. Maybe the experience supports the concept that all time exists simultaneously."

Betty Dishell, Farmington Hills, MI: "My first, unplanned experience with psychometry occurred twelve years ago. I was friendly with the couple who lived in the apartment downstairs from me, and they were aware of my interest in metaphysics. Mary Ellen was about six months pregnant when they decided to purchase a home for the growing family. They found a house they really liked, but it generated an uneasiness in Mary Ellen. She asked me to visit the house with them to 'get a feeling.'

"I agreed to go, but the appointment had to be canceled due to the realtor's illness. My neighbors were anxious to make a decision on the house, but the feelings of uneasiness continued. They asked if I would look at a picture of the place and give them my impressions. I was beginning to feel a little pressured that they were putting so much confidence in what I felt, but Mary Ellen assured me they would make their own decisions.

"I decided to go into an altered state, holding the picture to my third eye chakra, and see what happened. The deeper I went, the more contact I felt with this house. At first there was a swirling cloud and gradually that image was replaced by another that appeared to be a person. I realized that I was straining to see and decided to just focus gently on the outline of the person without trying to see anything else. As the image continued to form, I could see that it was a woman with dark hair who was pregnant, at about the same stage as Mary Ellen. At first I thought it was Mary Ellen and that I was seeing her in this new house, but as the image became more vivid, it was clearly someone else. In front of the woman was a baby crib with a baby in it. I could see the baby but not its face. At this point, I was unsure about what I was seeing. Then, as the woman quickly leaned over the crib and began gathering up the baby, I felt the baby was not hers and that she was stealing it. The image disappeared in an instant, leaving my mental screen blank and me with a feeling of great uneasiness.

"I wasn't sure how to interpret this and was even more unsure about giving my negative impressions to my friends. But they considered it important, so I told them what I saw. Mary Ellen was especially upset by what I had to say. It seemed to support her uneasy feelings about the house, though she had hoped that I would receive good impressions that would confirm their decision to buy the house.

"The more inquiries Mary Ellen made concerning the previous owners of the house, the more suspicious she and her husband became. Everyone seemed very secretive, so Mary Ellen expanded her investigation and finally uncovered the story. The previous owners were a young couple in their mid-twenties. They had no children, but the wife was about six months pregnant when she died under mysterious circumstances. Although they both seemed happy about the pregnancy, the wife was very depressed. One day, when the husband couldn't reach her by phone, he left work early and arrived home to find all the doors and windows bolted from the inside. He could get no response from his wife. The fire department broke down a side door and found the woman lying at the bottom of the basement stairs, her body badly broken and the baby almost ripped out of her.

"The husband was cleared of any suspicion, but there were many unanswered questions and much speculation among the neighbors about what happened. A simple fall down the stairs wouldn't have caused the physical damage she had sustained. Had she slashed herself with a knife, then jumped down the stairs? The husband was supposedly devastated by the loss of his wife. He left town, putting the house up for sale.

"Mary Ellen and her husband decided they were not interested in a house with such a negative background. I'm still not sure what it was that I picked up from the picture. Maybe the dead woman is still earthbound in the house and would have attempted to possess Mary Ellen's baby to replace the child she didn't have. But there again, maybe I was only seeing symbolic images of the past and the house would have been fine. I'll never know. But there is no doubt that, through a psychometric connection, I did receive psychic impressions that were supported by the investigation."

Pat Cochrell, Westlake, OR: *(Pat has worked as a professional astrologer and psychic for fifteen years, using the name "Rusty." The following are a few of her psychometry experiences.)* "I've learned over the past twenty-five years not to attempt to consciously interpret psychic impressions. Even if they make no sense to me, I verbalize whatever impressions I get. The symbols or impressions always turn out to have a specific meaning to the person I'm reading for. As an example, during a reading of a woman's ring, I received the sing-song words, "one potato, two potato, three." My client was very moved by this; it was a song-game her dead mother had played often with her as a child, and she'd been feeling very lonely for her mother. She laughed and said she felt very comforted and very happy to have heard the childhood tune again. The ring, now worn by her, had belonged to her mother.

"The object I psychometrize has to be worn by the subject for at least three or four weeks to get an effective reading for that person. New items haven't yet absorbed enough of the person's vibrations. Upon reading a beautiful turquoise and silver ring, I received nothing about the present owner, but described perfectly the Indian artisan who had crafted the ring. The owner had purchased it just two weeks earlier.

"While my husband and I were living in Las Vegas, I read a newspaper article about a missing little girl. Her family was asking for psychic help in locating their daughter. I decided to work on it, using the newspaper clipping as my psychometry focus. I figured I'd start there and see what I could get, then contact the family through the police for an article of the girl's clothing. I never got that far. The impressions I received just from the newspaper article had me in tears. I saw the little girl playing in the desert, crawling into a large corrugated metal culvert pipe and dying of heat exhaustion, with no foul play involved. Receiving the psychic impressions of the child's death upset me deeply. How could I bring myself to contact the family, even through the police, with such devastating news? How could I not? It was 3:00 P.M. when I did the reading. At 5:30 P.M., the news was on television. The body of the little girl had been found in the desert in a metal culvert. My dilemma had been resolved, and I decided I was not emotionally ready to deal with missing persons.

"When I do a psychometry reading, I hold the object in my hand, close my eyes, and pass it from hand to hand a few times, running my fingers over it; then the impressions begin to come. If the article/object is small enough, I work with it pressed lightly in the center on my forehead, on my third eye chakra. I begin a running commentary on what I am seeing in my mind, keeping the dialogue up until no more impressions come or I decide to end the reading. I prefer not to be interrupted until I have finished. Then, in response to questions, I briefly pick up the object again, close my eyes and try to receive the requested information.

"One thing I cannot read is a set of keys on a key ring. I can usually read an individual key if it's been off the key ring for an hour or two. A bunch of keys together results in jumbled mental static which I seem to absorb and have difficulty getting rid of.

"While doing a psychometry reading for a regular client, I had to tell him that I wasn't getting much information. He was unwillingly separated from his wife and three-year-old son and felt his life was shattered. The only picture I received clearly was in the distant future. He was living with his son, who appeared to be about ten years old. They were doing many recreational things: kite flying, camping, fishing. The odd thing was that his wife was not in these pictures at all. Not only wasn't she there visually, but her entire presence was totally missing. This was new to me and I did not know how to interpret it. When I attempted to shift the reading to the near future, I received only the same impressions of my client and his son in the distant future. These mental images were full and rich in detail; the two were very close and loving.

"Following the reading, the young man sadly shook his head and told me he could not believe that he and his son would be living together, as his wife was a caring and loving mother and would surely get custody of the boy. He left sad and broken-hearted, quite aimless in his despair.

"Two weeks later, he entered his estranged wife's apartment unannounced, found her in bed with another man, picked up his wife's handgun and shot her dead. He was tried and convicted of unpremeditated manslaughter and sentenced to prison. His parents were granted custody of his son. He will be eligible for parole just about the time his son will be ten years old."

Psychometry is the technique of holding an object and receiving impressions through the hands, the forehead, or the psychic center in your solar plexus (just below the breastbone). This physical contact allows you to tune in to the vibrations of the article, which are experienced by your sympathetic nervous system. The brain then amplifies and interprets the signals into "readable" information.

Metal holds psychometric emanations longer than other materials, but for my Sedona Psychic Seminar, I talk someone I know into giving me one of their well-worn T-shirts. It is then cut into three hundred pieces, which are distributed to the participants. In an altered state of consciousness, they are directed to perceive impressions about the owner of the shirt. The results are incredible—if I can convince them to trust their own mental impressions, they are amazingly successful.

The most easily read objects have been repeatedly used in the same activity or were involved in an emotional trauma that impregnated the molecules of the article with "memories." When impressions of the future are perceived by a psychometrist, he has moved beyond reading emanations and into a psychic mode. Future vibrations have obviously not yet been implanted in the object, but psychometry provided the "connection" for the psi impressions.

As with other psychic techniques, psychometry works best for most people while they are in an altered state of consciousness. Start out by holding the object in your left hand, palm up (right hand, palm down) as you go into the altered state. Once you have reached an adequate trance level, ask to receive impressions about the owner of the object. At this time, you may want to hold the object to your third eye. You must trust all the impressions you get—thoughts, feelings, and visualizations. Don't force it to happen, simply let it happen, and don't attempt to read too much into your perceptions.

In one of my first psychometry experiences, as part of a group experiment we each brought an item to be psychometrized. Each item was sealed in a package or envelope so we could not see what it was. Upon receiving my envelope, I went into an altered state, held the object to my third eye and perceived fantasy-like impressions of a woman in a white dress with long black hair, standing by the ocean. When I opened the envelope, I saw the printed reproduction of a painting of Jesus with long dark hair, wearing the traditional long white robe, standing beside a well.

CHAPTER

8

Spiritual Healing

Diana Ober, Gervais, OR: "My heart problems began in 1976. I had spent a long day on our cattle farm. I knew something was terribly wrong, for my heart raced, hesitated, and thumped out of rhythm for a terrifying half hour. I was put on medication but that only worsened the problem. At the age of forty-seven, I was praying like never before because I had too much to do to meet my Maker.

"Rest temporarily improved matters and I went back to work, but in 1979 my heart trouble returned. Now it took less and less to provoke cardiac arrhythmia, until just stooping down was enough to put my heart off its rhythm. Hospitals were out because we had no medical insurance and costs had soared beyond our reach.

"It was up to me to apply what I had learned from my spirit guide in meditation, which I did—every day, all day long, and often into the night. For the first six months of a two-and-a-half-year encounter with pain, I remained in a prone position, rising only long enough to eat and relieve myself. In my struggle to stay alive and get better, I learned what it is to be a survivor.

"I learned that four things, when used concurrently, will heal even critical ills: (1) Faith (determination to recover in spite of appearances); (2) Openness to guidance in meditation; (3) Life Energy; and (4) Persistence. My healing procedure is simpler to do than to describe. After going into an altered state of consciousness, I practice deep breathing, but as I exhale, I mentally say, 'H-m-m-m-m.' Let your tongue rest easily against the palate, behind the front teeth. At the start of your mental 'H-m-m-m-m,' make the tiniest mental grunt; and as you do, visualize a stream of energy flowing into and permeating your afflicted bodily organ. The tiny grunt gives just enough force to the 'H-m-m-m-m' to direct the Life Energy stream into the area you are treating. As you perform this, feel a warmth inundating the area.

"When you do this repeatedly, your mind becomes very quiet. Then it is time to start adding colors. I was given the colors to use by my guide: a brilliant electric blue for healing, silver or tan for calming, green for healing and normalizing, and yellow for all-around well-being. Pink and blue-reds are relaxing and energizing, purple and lavender also heal, while pink and salmon shades rejuvenate. The idea is to visualize the Life Energy stream in color, bathing and saturating the afflicted area with the prescribed hue. For me, during each session, the colors undergo changes from time to time, either on their own or at the direction of my guide.

"I've taught this technique to some friends, but few have been willing to do the sustained work required to get results. You have to keep at it, but the rewards are great; healing occurs that would otherwise be impossible. By the spring of 1982, my work began to pay off.

My heart was back in rhythm, but now I began a new battle. Because I had been flat on my back for so long, muscles in my chest and back had shortened, binding me under my arms and around my chest and back like iron bands. Nothing gave me relief, so I cut back on my heart-strengthening work and devoted the rest of my time to this new struggle. It took another year of work to experience any decrease in the pain.

"In the spring of 1983, I developed pneumonia, so I began to mentally work on my lungs. By May of that year I could take long walks and I felt I was returning to some level of health. It was at this time that I discovered your wonderful tapes, Dick. They gave me an enormous lift and ongoing help I use to this day. A neighbor told me of an art league in Woodburn, ten miles to the east, and I took up oil painting. Today, I'm the president of this thriving art league and actively involved in life.

"Many times over the years, I considered letting go and leaving the earth plane—it would have been so easy. But with the support of my spirit guide, I made the decision to remain and fulfill my long-term soul goals. The Life Energy remains at the center of my daily meditations, I am still making progress, and life is more meaningful than ever before."

Nancy Lopez, Berwyn, IL: "My world began to fall apart in 1980—my husband left me for another woman and I was diagnosed as having thyroid cancer. An operation removed the right side of my thyroid. In the months that followed, I met a wonderful man, remarried, and became pregnant. During the pregnancy a terrible kidney infection resulted in a badly scarred kidney. After my daughter was born, I had to go back into the hospital for another operation to remove more of my thyroid. To ensure that they got all the cancer the doctors also removed the lymph nodes in my throat area.

"A year later, in 1983, I had to go into the hospital again, this time for radiation treatments for cancerous cells in my throat. For a few years, my health was stable, but in 1986 the scar on my kidney caused a kidney stone. While in the hospital for a cystoscopy to remove the stone, the doctor accidentally tore a hole in my urethra, necessitating surgery. Due to the surgery, the bursa in my groin was destroyed, and I now walk with a slight limp and experience pain on my right side.

"After having so much happen in such a short time, I began to wonder if there was anything I could do to help myself get well and stay well. I was fortunate enough to find the book Love, Medicine and Miracles by Dr. Bernard Siegel—about how he uses meditation and creative visualization to help his cancer patients. After just a few weeks of using Siegel's techniques, I began to get in touch with my body and feel great.

"During this time, I also discovered your publication, Master of Life, and ordered some of your tapes, which I use religiously. By incorporating ideas from all of these sources, I have experienced a tremendous change in myself and my health. A recent biopsy to see if the cancer had returned did not even scare me. I knew my body was all right and the biopsy would prove to be negative. It was.

"When you conducted your Master of Life seminar in Chicago this year, my husband and I attended. I had always assumed my suffering was due to something terrible I'd done in a past life. I figured I was punishing myself for having been a terrible person. During one of the sessions, I was thrilled to make contact with my spirit guide. He informed me that I was inflicting all these terrible things upon myself, because I desired to strengthen my character for my chosen task. He told me that long ago, I had chosen to follow the way of the White Brotherhood, which I had never heard of before. Because of this choice, I would need all the strength and wisdom I was gaining in my current life as preparation for my future work.

"I figured I was either cracking up or my ego was doing all the talking. In my eyes, I'm quite an average, ordinary person. But since then my whole life has been changed and enriched, and I see the answers have always been in myself. I no longer need to wonder why, I just go inside and get my answers. I've begun to reach out more to people, and recently started working with a woman who puts out a newsletter for children with terminal illnesses. I enjoy doing this, and I am working on improving myself as best I can in this lifetime. I've learned I can control my pain through meditation, and I'm learning how to control my health.

"I get a lot of ridicule for my beliefs from those around me, but my experiences have given me a new perspective on life and on the suffering that is part of existence on the earth plane. There is a direction to my life now and I'm a happy, spiritual, and *healthy* person. I'm closer to God than ever before and I am glad to be alive."

Mary Vinson, Waimanalo, HI: "Last year, I ordered your Healing Acceleration tape. I used it and then passed it on to my son who found it helped alleviate a condition for which the doctors could find no logical reason. This past January, I suffered excruciating pain; the diagnosis was gallstones. Naturally, the doctors wanted me on the operating table as soon as possible. Fortunately, I was able to stall for time so that when the X rays were taken, the gallstones, polyps, and soft tissue mass previously seen in two ultra-sound film examinations were no longer there. I cannot say that using your tape two to three times a day was the only reason for my healing, but I know that it was an enormously important part of it."

Marian K. Rush, Spokane, WA: "Shortly before her twelfth birthday, my daughter Donna exhibited a personality transformation that was to change her life, and the lives of everyone around her. In an incredibly short time, she went from being the 'golden girl' in her school and everyone's best friend to being a dirty, careless, amoral, and pale shadow of her former self. Her moral standards seemed to disappear overnight as she slid into lying, cheating, crimes of arson, theft, drug abuse, alcohol abuse, promiscuity, and vagrancy.

"Running away from home, she lived with a steady succession of parasitic boyfriends in dirty dumps, surviving by stealing and drug dealing. Over these two years, she did, however, get in touch with me from time to time. I was determined not to give up on her and constantly assured her that I loved her and wanted her back. She'd come home on a few occasions, staying a few days before disappearing again. It broke my heart to see her so thin, sick, and dirty. I tried to help her clean herself up, gain some weight, and restore her health during these brief stays at home.

"In the fall of 1987, she tried a week of school but soon disappeared to be picked up for vagrancy two weeks later in Idaho. In November she was badly beaten by one of her boyfriends and all of her belongings were stolen. She returned home for a brief stay before leaving again. I was in the depths of despair and found relief only in my meditation and participation in a group channeling effort. In a channeling session, the name 'Shannon' was mentioned, and I recalled that my daughter used to get phone calls for Shannon. She explained that Shannon was her 'street name.'

"In the channeling, I was told that Shannon was a displaced spirit, a young girl who had met death but hadn't found her way to the light. She still lived vicariously through a series of young, impressionable girls. In searching for proof, I found some old school papers in Donna's room. One paper was a personality profile. Some of the questions were answered sensibly in very neat handwriting, and then crossed over and answered in a tough, rude manner in very sloppy writing. If ever two personalities were evident, it was in that paper!

"My spirit guide told me to tell Shannon to go to the light, but it just didn't work. During the few opportunities I had to talk with Donna about Shannon, she defended Shannon, saying that she didn't want to get rid of her. There was obviously a strong bond between the two girls.

"I was now intensifying my meditation periods and enhancing the effects with crystals. A dear friend was in the hospital for treatment of a rare blood ailment. Her son phoned me in tears, saying that she couldn't produce platelets. Her count was down to 82 and she wasn't expected to live. Somehow I was guided into a perfect meditation and I 'traveled' to the hospital. I stood beside her bed and watched her sleep, and then I begged, pleaded, and coerced her circulatory system to start producing more platelets. She was too good a person to lose at the young age of thirty-five, and I poured my soul into that procedure. When I came out of my meditation with the crystal still firmly clutched in my hand, I felt very good about it all and slept well. Early the next morning, I learned my friend's platelet count had soared to over 400.

"Soon after this experience, I decided if I could help heal a friend I might be able to help my daughter. So, on a Saturday afternoon, I settled myself in my favorite chair, with my crystal firmly clasped in my left hand. I placed my left hand over my heart and covered it with my right hand. When the crystal was pulsating in the same rhythm as my heart, I asked to astrally travel to find my daughter. Soon I was in the living room of a dirty house with Donna sitting in a chair, looking preoccupied and distraught. There were two sullen young men in the room, but she was ignoring them. A glowing black area on Donna's chest was not exactly a hole, but a vulnerable spot. I didn't hesitate a moment, and went right into her body and soul, where I came face to face with Shannon.

"Shannon was distant and resistant, facing me in a belligerent manner. I talked to her reasonably, telling her that she would have to go to the light. 'No!' she said. I tried again, explaining what had happened, and that she shouldn't be here. Again, the stubborn stare and arrogant manner. Looking her straight in the eye so I wouldn't lose her, I searched my mind for a new tactic. I hadn't come this far to be buffaloed by a snotty teenager! Then it struck me—I had been talking to her on an adult-to-adult level, while she was really a scared and stubborn child. The next portion of our conversation went like this:

"Me: 'You really have to go.'

"Shannon: 'I don't want to. I like it here.'

"Me: 'But you're hurting a lot of people.'

"Shannon: 'Tough shit!'

"Me: 'Are you scared?'

"Shannon: 'No.' (pause) 'Yes.'

"Me: 'I'll go with you. I'll hold your hand.'

"Shannon: 'You'll go with me?'

"Me: 'Yes, I will.'

"Shannon: 'Aren't you scared?'

"Me: 'Yes, I am, but I'll do it.'

"Shannon: 'Hold my hand.'

"At this point, we found ourselves hand in hand on the brink of a very large meadow. On the distant horizon, a small disk of a dark blue color rose into the sky and spiraled toward us. When it was about a hundred feet over our heads, it exploded harmlessly.

This phenomenon was repeated two more times. Then we were floating hand in hand through the sky, higher and higher, and I was strangely unafraid. Soon a light appeared in the distance. I had heard so much about it over the years. It is lovely beyond description, perfectly round, in beautiful hues of red, orange, yellow, and white. As we neared the center, I was momentarily anxious, wondering if I would ever come out of it, but there was no time to worry. The deed was done.

"Once inside the light, the experience was similar to being on a fast-moving train, except instead of scenery or countryside to look at there were lines of people on both sides. They looked at us with some curiosity. At last the fast journey stopped in a kind of tunnel. We walked slowly toward the end of the tunnel, seemingly directed by some other force than our own sense of direction. I saw a woman sitting on the ground, holding a small infant in her arms. She was wearing a long, hooded, maroon dress, and seemed to be in the depths of sadness, staring listlessly at the ground.

"As we approached, she looked up at us, and a beautiful smile illuminated her face. I thought she was the loveliest woman I had ever seen. She stood up, looked straight into my eyes and touched my arm, saying, 'Thank you for bringing my daughter back to me.'

I said, 'I want my daughter back too.'

"If there was a return journey, it has been blocked from my conscious memory. I opened my eyes in my own living room and was surprised to note that only twenty minutes had passed. In the days that followed, I knew in my heart that I had accomplished something good. I knew I couldn't expect immediate results; it would take some time for my daughter's natural intelligence and common sense to assert themselves and guide her back home.

"The next few months were rocky. It was the same old pattern of Donna coming home and leaving, but now with longer and longer stays at home. In April 1988, she returned home, she says, 'to stay.' A special summer school program is currently preparing her for a return to high school in the fall."

Your state of mind, more than anything else, determines how healthy you are. Even ancient Hermetic philosophy states that a negative mental state is a breeding ground for disease. In other words, most health problems are emotionally induced. They start mentally and become physical.

The good news is, what mind has created, mind can change. Everything we experience is karmic—beginning with thoughts. And from a karmic perspective, you and you alone are responsible for absolutely everything that has ever happened to you. When it comes to healing, since you are the cause, you will ideally be active rather than passive in the healing process.

According to metaphysical teachings, the four energy bodies of man simultaneously coincide in space. You are familiar with your *physical body* existing on the *physical plane*. Next highest is the *vital body* existing on the *etheric plane*. This body maintains the physical pattern but remains perfect, and is thus a model for the physical. It regulates healing. Next is the *astral body* existing on the *astral plane*. We use our astral body after physical death. Next is the *mental body,* which exists on the *spiritual plane*. When you have evolved beyond the need of reincarnation on the physical plane, you will use this body.

Spiritual healing uses the vital body as a perfect model and considers the importance of all four bodies in activating and maintaining the subtle energy system. The place to begin is with an examination of why your life isn't working. Forgiveness is a key factor in healing—forgiving yourself and everyone else. Behavior, attitude, and life-style are also extremely important. Let's begin with an altered-state-of-consciousness session in which you search for cause, explore forgiveness, and then use a metaphysical technique for self-healing.

Exploration and Self-Healing Script

(Begin with the induction technique described in Chapter 2.) "I am now relaxed and at ease and feeling at peace, balanced, and harmonious. And I am ready to explore self-healing. Sometimes to be healed of mental, emotional, or physical problems, people need to resolve a negative relationship . . . or stop blaming . . . or forgive someone in their past, possibly themselves. Or maybe they need to release a fear, or even heal their relationship with the Divine as they understand it.

"Now I will be totally open to the first impression that comes into my mind. Is there someone I need to forgive, including myself?" *(Pause.)*

"What about blame? Blame is self-pity and incompatible with karma. Whom do I blame?" *(Pause.)*

"Do I need to release a fear?" *(Pause.)*

"If so, what is the cause of the fear? I will go back as far into my past as necessary to find the cause. This includes memories of other lifetimes. On the count of three, vivid impressions will begin to come in. One . . . two . . . three." *(Pause.)*

"When I know the cause, can I forgive myself and others who were involved? And can I release myself from the disharmonious effect?" *(Pause.)*

"Attitude, behavior, and life-style are other important factors in healing. So, first, let's look at my attitudes toward life. Is my attitude defensive? Is it aloof? Do I resent others? Do I feel any anger? It is time to explore my attitudes in regard to all the fear-based emotions." *(Pause.)*

"What is behind this attitude?" *(Pause.)*

"Are my attitudes working against me?" *(Pause.)*

"Now, let's look at my behavior. Are there areas of my life in which I do things that cause me to lose self-esteem? Maybe not standing up for my rights, or saying yes when I want to say no. Are there things I should do and don't? Do I do things that cause me to feel bad about myself?" *(Pause.)*

"Have I done things I am punishing myself for?" *(Pause.)*

"What about my life-style and my diet? Do they work from a perspective of physical health?" *(Pause.)*

"What does my higher mind want me to do about blaming . . . and forgiving . . . and attitudes . . . and behavior . . . and life-style . . . and diet? My higher mind, or spirit guide, will speak to me in thought language. On the count of three, this awareness will come to me. One . . . two . . . three." *(Long pause.)*

"Can I forgive myself? Can I forgive others? Can I stop blaming and let go of negativity? If I can, I am ready to accept healing. I need to meditate on this." *(Long pause.)*

"My body is composed of trillions of atoms held together by a vibrational rate and electromagnetism. When these atoms are disarranged, disease can result. But my etheric body always maintains its original perfection, so I can use my perfect etheric body as a model for healing. I am now going to visualize my etheric body in its perfection and extending just beyond my physical body." *(Pause.)*

"And it is now time to unblock my natural flow of healing energy, which is abundant. Once again, I imagine a light coming down from above, only this time it is the healing ray of the Universal light energy—an intense blue light. An intense, shimmering, iridescent blue light coming down from above and entering my crown chakra of spirituality. As it flows, it unblocks my natural healing energy." *(Use focused visualization to see the light. Feel it flowing through you and imagine its healing effect. If you are dealing with a disease, such as cancer, do a guided fantasy in which you visualize first the cancer cells, then the white blood cells destroying the cancer cells, and finally the healthy tissue that remains after the disease is cured. Do this visualization twice a day.)*

"Feel it! The blue healing ray is flowing through me, bringing up the healing, pranic vibrations. I am healing, I am healed. I am healing, I am healed. The more I think loving, compassionate, positive thoughts, the more I raise the healing vibrations." *(Spend several minutes visualizing the intense blue light flowing through you and silently in your mind chant a mantra: "I am healing, I am healed.")*

"I am open to healing. I forgive myself and I forgive everyone in my past. The healing has begun. I am healing, I am healed." *(Awaken)*

Occasionally, people will feel worse on the day after an intense healing session. This is part of the cleansing and the discomfort will pass within twenty-four hours.

The goal of the next session is to heal someone else. Step 1: Ask the other person the questions you answered in the self-healing session, if they are appropriate. Step 2: Discuss your subject's healing needs. Step 3: Have your subject lie down on a massage table or on the floor. Use the "stroking" technique to cleanse their etheric aura: Hold your hands about two inches above them—within their etheric field—and then with your hands apart and fingers spread, make long, fluid passes over their entire body, clearing it for the

positive healing energy which you will soon transmit.
Step 4: Sitting on a chair or on the floor beside your
subject, enter an altered state of consciousness.

One-On-One Healing Script

(Induction first.) "And I am now relaxed and at ease,
in balance and harmony, and I am ready to serve as a
Divine healing channel for another in need of this
energy. (Name of your subject), it is time for you to
open to the healing. Unblock and open. And I want
you to visualize your etheric body. Your etheric body
always maintains its original perfection, so use it as a
model for your physical body. Visualize your etheric
body and open. . . .

"And I now draw down the healing ray of Universal
life energy. The Divine God-light. It is a shimmering,
iridescent blue beam descending from above and
entering the crown chakra of spirituality on the top of
my head. I feel the light. I experience the light. I
manifest the light with the unlimited power of my
mind, and it now flows through my body and mind."
(Pause and use visualization to intensify the blue light.)

"I have the power to heal with my hands, and the
light is now beginning to concentrate in both of my
hands at the same time. Flowing into my shoulders,
down into my arms, and concentrating in my hands.
As it does my hands are getting hotter and hotter . . .
hotter and hotter. And as I build the energy, (Name),
you are to concentrate upon forgiveness. Forgive
yourself. Forgive others. It is time to let go of the
negativity and to believe in this healing. Remember
Jesus' words, 'Your belief has set you free.'" *(Concentrate all of your energy upon visualizing and feeling the
blue light concentrating in the palms of your hands.
Tell yourself, 'As the energy builds, my hands are*

getting hotter and hotter . . . hotter and hotter.' Imagine them getting hotter and it will become reality. When you feel the energy is peaking, lay your hands upon your subject where the healing is needed.)

"I am a channel for Divine healing energy. I now freely transfer my energy to you. Accept this loving gift and be healed now. Allow the energy to flow freely through your body and mind, healing you mentally, healing you emotionally, healing you physically. You are healing, you are healed. Perceive yourself as healed." *(Long pause. Then awaken.)*

As the healing channel, be sure you take time after the session to shake off any disharmonious vibrations you may have picked up. Spread your fingers wide and shake them as if you were shaking off water.

Balancing and energizing your seven energy chakras is considered by many metaphysicians to be an essential step in healing. Sometimes this session alone can resolve physical, mental, or emotional problems. Because of the time required, it is suggested that you make your own tape of the script.

Chakra Balancing and Energizing Script

(Induction.) "I am now relaxed and at ease and centered upon achieving my goals. I am at peace and feel in balance and in harmony. A quietness of spirit permeates my body and mind, and in a moment, I am going to begin to balance and energize my chakras—the seven energy force centers that exist on the surface of my etheric double and influence all aspects of my life.

"The chakras open naturally as I evolve spiritually; in balancing and energizing them, I assure myself greater health and vitality. So I begin by imagining a beam of bright white light coming down from above and entering the top of my head—a shimmering iridescent light, entering the crown chakra of spirituality. I see the light, I create it, I intensify it . . . and so it is. This is the universal light of life energy—the God light. And I experience feelings of warmth and well-being as the light enters my crown chakra.

"Visualize the crown chakra as a beautiful lotus flower within a lotus flower. The inner lotus has sixteen petals and is white and gold; the outer lotus is violet and contains 960 petals. It rotates and radiates and is the seat of my highest vibrational energy. My crown chakra represents the 'I AM I,' and full development of this energy center will result in a blissful union with the Divine source lying latent in my consciousness. To fully develop this chakra is to become totally aware of my true self.

"And I now sense the balancing and energizing that is taking place within me. I visualize the colors of my crown chakra and experience an inner balancing and energizing as the white light of life energy spins through this vortex. Balancing and energizing. Balancing and energizing. *(Pause for visualization.)* And my crown chakra of spirit is now balanced and energized.

"And the light energy is now moving on down into my brow chakra, located in the center of my forehead. This is my third eye chakra and it can be visualized as a beautiful rotating lotus flower with ninety-six petals that are blue violet in color. It radiates and is the seat of the mind, so it relates to the power of thought. As I develop this chakra, I develop my ability to think reality into existence. And I now sense the balancing and energizing that is taking place within me. I visualize the blue violet color and experience a balancing and energizing as the white light of life energy spins through this energy center. Balancing and energizing. Balancing and energizing. *(Pause for visualization.)* And my brow chakra of thought is now balanced and energized.

"And the light is now moving on down into my throat chakra, located on my spine at the level of my throat. This chakra is to be visualized as a beautiful rotating lotus flower with sixteen petals, silvery-blue in color. It radiates, and as the first chakra of the five physical senses, represents the qualities of ether—the pure essence of space, which allows the four lower elements of air, fire, water, and earth to be formed. It also enables us to sense sounds and voices. And I now feel the balancing and energizing that is taking place with me. I visualize the silvery-blue color and experience an inner balancing and energizing as the white light of life energy spins through this energy vortex. Balancing and energizing. Balancing and energizing. *(Pause for visualization.)* And my throat chakra of ether is now balanced and energized.

"And the light is now moving on down into my heart chakra, located on my spine at the level of my heart. Visualize this chakra as a beautiful rotating lotus flower with twelve petals and golden in color. It radiates and represents the qualities of air in my personality—mobility, gentleness, and lightness. It relates to my relationships and to the physical sense of touch. And I now feel the balancing and energizing that is taking place within me. I visualize the golden color and experience an inner balancing and energizing as the white light of life energy spins through this energy vortex. Balancing and energizing. Balancing and energizing. *(Pause for visualization.)* And my heart chakra of air is now balanced and energized.

"And the light is now moving on down into my solar plexus chakra, located on my spine at the level of my navel. This chakra is to be visualized as a beautiful lotus flower with ten rotating petals that are several shades of red. It radiates and represents the qualities of fire—expansiveness, warmth, and joy, My eyesight and the assimilation of food are governed by the activity of this chakra. The more this chakra is stimulated, the more energy I will derive from my food. And I now sense the balancing and energizing that are taking place within me. I visualize the many shades of red and experience an inner balancing and energizing as the white light of life energy spins through this energy vortex. Balancing and energizing. Balancing and energizing. *(Pause for visualization.)* And my solar plexus chakra of fire is now balanced and energized.

"And the light is now moving on down into my spleen chakra, located on my spine a little below my solar plexus chakra. This chakra is to be visualized as a beautiful lotus flower with six petals, and each petal is a different color—red, orange, yellow, green, blue, and violet. It radiates and represents the qualities of water, governing energy as fluidity. The spleen center is associated with the fluid functions of urine and semen. It lubricates the body internally while also governing the sense of taste. And I now sense the balancing and energizing that is taking place within me. I visualize the many colors and experience an inner balancing and energizing as the white light of life energy spins through this energy vortex. Balancing and energizing. Balancing and energizing. *(Pause for visualization.)* And my spleen chakra of water is now balanced and energized.

"And the light is now moving on down into my root chakra, located at the very base of my spine. And this chakra is to be visualized as a beautiful lotus flower with four rotating petals that are red and orange in color. It radiates and represents the qualities of earth, such as solidity. This earth vibration keeps my feet planted firmly on the ground, and this chakra governs the solid elements of my body—bones, teeth, and nails. It is associated with my sense of smell . . . and I now feel the balance and energizing taking place within me. I visualize the red orange color and experience an inner balancing and energizing as the white light of life energy spins through this energy vortex. Balancing and energizing. Balancing and energizing. *(Pause for visualization.)* And the root chakra of earth is now balanced and energized.

"My seven chakras are now balanced and energized, and I am aware that the pranic breath of life is closely connected with my chakras. When breathing in I spiritualize and regenerate myself. With the in breath the life energy is drawn upward to the higher chakras, while the out breath channels energies downwards into the lower chakras, or world of the senses.

"And now, for a couple minutes, as I breathe in, I visualize my spiritual goals . . . and as I breathe out, I visualize myself successfully coping with the world of matter and the senses. *(Pause at least two minutes for visualization.)*

"And I am now relaxed and at ease, and I sense the quietness of spirit that permeates my body and mind. My energy chakras are now balanced and energized, and I will soon awaken filled with aliveness and joy. I will be centered and at peace with myself, the world and everyone in it.

"All right, once more I visualize my chakras as the white light of life energy moves back up my spine, beginning with my root chakra . . . a four-petaled rotating lotus flower, red and orange in color . . . and on up into my spleen chakra, a six-petaled rotating lotus flower of six colors . . . and on up into my solar plexus chakra, a ten-petaled rotating lotus flower that is several shades of red . . . and on up into my heart chakra, a twelve-petaled rotating lotus flower of golden color . . . and on up into my throat chakra, a

sixteen-petaled rotating lotus flower of silvery-blue
. . . and on up into my brow, or third eye chakra, a
ninety-six-petaled rotating lotus flower, blue violet in
color . . . and on up into my crown chakra of spirituality, a lotus flower within a lotus flower—the inner
gold and white flower made up of sixteen petals, the
outer one containing 960 violet petals.

"And I have now completed the balancing and
energizing of the seven energy force centers that are
the essence of my being. The result of this balancing
and energizing will be expanded awareness, increased
vitality, and improving health." *(Awaken.)*

CHAPTER

9

Group Healing

Kay Thomas, Albuquerque, NM: "In your last Albuquerque seminar, I stood in the middle circle of the healing circles. For several months, I had experienced extreme pain and numbness in my back and left leg from sciatic nerve damage. It hasn't given me any trouble since I walked out of the hotel ballroom that evening. Many thanks to all the wonderful people who generated the energy and to you for directing it."

Helen Fredericks, Pasadena, CA: "My heart condition is the result of a birth defect, but it wasn't until 1973, when I was twenty-four, that doctors at UCLA Medical Center decided to do a heart catheter and find out exactly what was wrong. They discovered that I had an arterial-septal defect—a hole between the top two chambers of my heart—plus the valve between the right top and bottom chambers was deformed. They didn't recommend surgery at the time, but said it would probably be inevitable at a later date.

"The doctors followed my case for seven years but there was no change, and I stopped seeing them in 1980. About this time I started attending your seminars, and during the healing circles I began visualizing the hole in my heart closing. At first, I really didn't put much faith into it, but would always send the healing power to my heart.

"In 1984, at the Sedona Psychic Seminar, I really 'felt' the healing energy, and concentrated it into my heart. From then on, during the healing circles, I visualized the hole getting smaller and smaller. Last year, I decided it was time to start visualizing it as closed. A portion of my mental movies include the doctor telling me that the hole in my heart was closed and no longer a problem.

"Then, in August of 1987, I began to notice my energy was very low, I wasn't feeling well, and was experiencing chest pains. After trying unsuccessfully to treat it with medication, my doctor recommended another heart catheter to see what areas were causing the problem. In the final analysis, they found no arterial-septal defect. The hole had completely closed. The odds of something like this happening are incalculable.

"The right valve is deformed, as is the right side of my heart, yet the pressures and performance of the heart is normal. The doctor couldn't explain this either. He felt my initial symptoms were from exhaustion. (My pattern is to go until I'm exhausted and then sleep forty-eight hours to catch up. This time, I'd been too busy to take the time to rest.)

"I've now changed my eating habits and am getting more exercise. As a result, my doctor feels I am at no more risk of a heart attack or future heart surgery than anyone with a normal heart. Personally, I am convinced that the power of the healing circles closed the hole and is the reason it functions normally. So, thanks again for doing those healing circles at the end of each seminar! They do accomplish miracles!"

* * *

For years, I have experimented in my seminars with group techniques for mental, physical, and spiritual healing. These were always most effective when the synergistic energy of the group was activated. Synergy, in this sense, means the uniting of individual energies to generate a far greater effect than one person could have acting independently.

When you explore metaphysical energy, you discover that two and two do not necessarily add up to four. The combined energy of four like-minded people could add up to eight, twelve, or sixteen—and possibly more. In my seminars I ask two or three hundred people to form circles within circles, then direct them to draw down the light and begin to generate healing energy and move it around the circles, in their left hand and out their right, "increasing, intensifying, accelerating, and expanding." And everyone in the room feels it. They know it is happening.

Those most in need of healing are instructed to be in the inner circles and at the proper time I instruct all participants as follows: "And now, with a deep and compassionate love for all mankind, we ask Thy divine assistance in our endeavor to heal those in our circles who most need this healing. We combine and magnify our group energy and send it to those in the center and ask, in Thy name, that they be healed. Send them the energy . . . AND BE HEALED NOW! BE HEALED NOW! Those of you in the center of the circle, take this light and energy that is being sent to you and use it to heal yourself in God's name now! BE HEALED NOW! BE HEALED NOW!"

There are always healings. Sometimes the problem disappears over the following weeks. Often the cure is very dramatic and happens immediately, as in the case of a middle-age woman with a throat tumor. At the end of the healing circle, she gulped, swallowed hard, and the tumor was gone. She later reported that her doctor verified the disappearance of the tumor. "He was in a state of disbelief," she reported.

Mental healing is another result of participation in the circles. Anxiety, fears, phobias, guilt, and the pain of loss are often eased or eliminated by those willing to explore the potential of synergistic energy.

Anyone who wants to explore the potential of synergistic healing should not try to do it by contacting me or attending my seminars. I do no individual counseling and I don't end all my seminars with a healing circle. Instead, I suggest that you practice these techniques with your own friends or local metaphysical organizations. The following techniques are not the only way to synergize healing energy; they are simply the ones I have found to be most effective. The process obviously reflects my own background and point of view—a combination of occultism, psychology, and Zen. If you relate more to Christianity or Christ Consciousness, then you'll probably want to alter the process to reflect your own beliefs.

One of the secrets of a successful healing circle is to generate a "sense of oneness" in a large group of like-minded people. I've found this is easier if I wait until the afternoon of the second day of a two-day seminar. By then, the participants have shared many common experiences and a camaraderie exists, a warmth and sense of unity that easily translates to the combined efforts of the healing circle.

The technique works with any number of people, but I personally prefer to have at least one hundred. In my seminars, I usually direct two or three hundred people, and this expands the energy many, many times. I don't know how much it is intensified—possibly multiplied three or four times, or even squared or cubed—but four times the energy of three hundred people would equal the focused healing energy of twelve hundred people. This would mean that twelve hundred metaphysical people are all drawing down the God light, the universal light of life energy, and expanding and intensifying it. No wonder we get healings.

Before sharing the script, let me give you the invocation I use as part of most spiritual seminar activities.

The White Light Opening and Protective Invocation/Ritual

"To Thee, O God, be the kingdom, and the power, and the glory, unto the ages of ages . . . Amen." (This is part of many esoteric teachings from the Kabala to the Order of the Golden Dawn.) "I seek Thy protection from all things seen and unseen, all forces and all elements. In Thy Divine Name, I open to the light. I offer my body, my mind, and my spirit to the light. Let Thy Divine Will and mine be as one. I seek to expand the light within and I seek a tranquil mind and harmony with the Divine Law. I thank Thee in advance for the unfolding visions, spiritual awareness, and healing that awaits me. As it is above, so it is below. I ask these things in Thy Name. I beseech it and I mark it . . . and so it is."

All participants stand in a circle holding hands—left hand up to receive and right hand down to give out. Ideally, the participants would clasp a crystal between their cupped hands to further enhance the healing energy. If many people are present, stand in circles within circles. Those most in need of healing should be in the innermost circles. The lights should be low—candlelight is ideal. Recite prayers or a metaphysical invocation such as the one above. The person directing the session must have a good sound system so his voice will be heard above the group as they chant the OM. A second microphone is needed for a female voice to lead the OM. I also use inspiring New Age music, and for the finale, I switch to very powerful music before reciting the last few lines of the script.

Because the participants have been exploring together in an altered state of consciousness for two days, a light trance state can be easily induced by a gentle, repetitive voice as they stand in concentric circles. This will increase the effectiveness of the session.

I created the healing circle in 1978 and have used it in my seminars ever since because the participants never get tired of what is for many of them an incredible experience. Over the years, numerous seminar leaders have borrowed it or varied it to meet their particular needs. Although I basically adhere to the following script, I also improvise a lot, to drive the energy higher. The entire process, once the participants have formed their circles, can take anywhere from fifteen to forty minutes.

The Healing Circle Script

"Hold hands now, close your eyes, and center yourselves by slowing down your thoughts and allowing the quietness of spirit to come in. Breathe deeply and sense the oneness in the room. Feel the balance and harmony. We are one mind, one essence. And we now draw down the power of the circles. We draw down the light from above and it encompasses these circles—shimmering, iridescent, white God Light. We invoke the light and it becomes reality. And our power is doubled, tripled, quadrupled by our shared energy as we draw down the light. We experience the light, we become the light, we radiate the light, and we invoke the blessing of the source of the light." *(Pause for a minute of silence.)*

"Let this light of balance and harmony bring healing to all who stand within the aura. And now feel the energy of the circles expanding . . . flowing through the circles, in your left hand and out your right. Expanding, accelerating, rotating through the circles, intensifying! Feel the energy increasing. Let's all sway back and forth with the increasing energy as we intone the OM together. The OM is all sound and silence throughout time, the roar of eternity and essence of pure being. It invokes the ALL that is otherwise inexpressible." *(A female voice leads the group OM, and I begin to shout into the microphone, "Bring down the light and bring up the power of the OM." If the participants are not OMing very loud, I simply say, "Louder. Intone the OM louder. Increase the energy.")*

"And the energy continues to flow through the circles, into your left hand and out of your right, accelerating, building, increasing, intensifying. And now, as you hold your hands even tighter, feel a heat in your hands as the healing energy intensifies. Feel the pulsations in your hands. And your hands are getting hotter and hotter as the light and energy builds and intensifies. And now, EXPERIENCE THE LIGHT AND ENERGY, HEALING YOUR BODY AND MIND. Visualize yourself as healed physically, and allow the light and energy to cleanse and heal you mentally. Let go of the sorrow and the suffering, the worry and the blame. Allow the light and energy to cleanse your mind of negativity. From this moment on, you are a channel for the light, and you rise above all negative earthly concerns. From this moment on, you will respond to all situations as your loving Masters would respond: with love and compassion . . . and with a tranquil mind." *(Period of silence while the group continues to sway and intone the OM. During this period, I will say short, encouraging things to the participants: "Visualize yourself as healed.*

Imagine you are healed. It is time to forgive yourself and allow the healing to happen. As we have learned this weekend, wisdom erases karma. Your physical problems and diseases and your state of mind are your karma. Isn't it time to let go of this karma and forgive yourself? You can walk out the doors of this hotel ballroom healed, if you will only accept the healing.")

"And now, with a deep and compassionate love for all mankind, we ask Thy Divine assistance in our endeavor to heal those in our circle who most need this healing. We combine and magnify our group energy and send it to those in the center and ask, in Thy Name, that they be healed. Everyone . . . send your energy into the center circles. Those of you in the center circles, TAKE THIS ENERGY AND BE HEALED NOW. We have the power and energy of hundreds and hundreds in this room, and you have an incredible opportunity for healing. So take this energy that is being sent to you and use it to heal yourself in God's name now! BE HEALED NOW! BE HEALED NOW!" *(Period of silence while the group continues to sway and intone the OM.)*

"And now, let's project the healing light and energy of this powerful circle out into the world to those who are in need. Send it out now. If you have a loved one in need of healing, send them this light and love and energy and perceive them as being healed now! SEE THEM IN YOUR MIND AS HEALED." *(Improvise words of your own to send the energy out to those who are part of a current world crisis . . . and simply to help heal the earth and all her people.)*

(Silence with music playing in the background and the participants OMing. End with resolution music such as "Also Sprach Zarathustra," used in the sound-track of the movie 2001.)

"We invoke the power of the circles in Thy divine name. We ask it, we beseech it, we mark it . . . and so it is! Go in peace and do your best." *(Let the soothing music continue to play and keep the lights low.)*

I immediately leave the hotel ballroom while the participants are still swaying and enjoying the incredible energy. If I remain in the room at the end, the participants will all crowd around the stage to ask questions and say good-byes. If I'm not there, they will turn to each other, which is as it should be.

Sometimes I will leave the lights low, the music playing, and I won't end with, "Go in peace and do your best." On such occasions the group has often continued to sway and OM for half an hour or more before finally ending the session on their own.

SECTION

II

Human Potential Awareness & Techniques

The human potential movement is a quest by masses of people to become all they are capable of being. It is more a process than a philosophy, and combines logic, Zen and metaphysics with self-awareness and self-acceptance. The primary goals: 1) The acceptance of total responsibility for your life; 2) The acceptance of "what is"; 3) Mental detachment from negativity; 4) Conscious choice of harmonious viewpoints.

CHAPTER

10

The Fear-Based
Emotions

Now that you've used esoteric techniques to find some of your own answers within, it is time to explore the next level of awareness. No matter what enlightening discoveries you've made, the only way to truly *end suffering, attain peace of mind,* and *become spiritually enlightened* is to secure freedom *of* the self and freedom *from* the self.

Bondage manifests externally as oppression of all kinds—from relationships to religions, from poverty to an unfulfilling career. Internally we are held in bondage to the incessant babbling of our mind about guilt, envy, anger, greed, possessiveness, hate, selfishness, jealousy, repression, anxiety, insecurity, frustration, need for approval, resistance, revenge, inhibitions, egotism, resentment, need to control, blame, and all the other fear-based emotions.

Absolute freedom can only be attained through *detachment from negativity.* Conscious detachment is a matter of allowing negative (fear-based) thoughts and emotions to flow through your mind without affecting you. Detachment comes as the result of awareness, not technique. The best way to begin attaining that awareness is by exploring your suffering.

The new Zen-based psychotherapies assert that unhappy and neurotic people are not satisfying their needs and have developed negative patterns of thinking. Actions follow thinking, so the end result is suffering. Since there is no way to heal a mind, medical therapy is of no value. Unless you need hospital treatment or prescription drugs, all a mental health counselor can do is to alter your viewpoint or make you aware of your unconscious programming. The rest is up to you. As I stressed in the first section of this volume: *Wisdom erases karma.*

Wisdom begins with learning to choose to behave in ways that will result in harmony instead of disharmony. Basically, this is the ability to reason. A primary goal of contemporary therapies is to convince an individual to be more responsible and realistic regarding short-term sacrifices versus long-term goals.

Everyone has the need to love and be loved, to feel worthwhile to ourselves and to others. If either of these needs is unfulfilled, your life won't work as well as it would if these needs were satisfied. Regarding the need to love: you must be involved with other people —one at a very minimum. You must love that person and feel loved in return. If you don't have this critical person in your life, a basic need is unfulfilled, and mental and emotional symptoms may result.

To feel worthwhile to yourself and others, you must maintain a satisfactory standard of behavior. This means correcting yourself when you recognize faults and mistakes. If your ego-self's conduct is below your standard, you must correct it or you are likely to experience mental and emotional symptoms, just as if you had no one to love or no one who loves you.

Two of the goals in my Master of Life Seminars are to see if you are blocking love and to encourage immediate changes in *behavior,* thus assisting you to fulfill your needs. It isn't even important to change how you feel about something if you are willing to change what you are doing—it has been well documented that a change in *attitude* will follow. Karma means action! Solid change begins with action.

Nothing about yourself can be changed until it is first recognized and accepted. So, first you must learn to *process* yourself, a human-potential term for asking yourself the right questions. Answers are never difficult when you stop avoiding the questions. Five questions are the key to self-processing:

1. What is the real fear?
2. Is this fear valid?
3. What needs do I have that are not being met?
4. What am I doing that creates disharmony?
5. What immediate actions can I take to create more harmony?

The Five Questions Using Jealousy as an Example

WHAT IS THE REAL FEAR? You are extremely jealous and possessive of your mate. The real fear might be that you feel you are unworthy and will someday lose your mate to someone who offers more.

IS THIS FEAR VALID? Examine the idea of being unworthy. Do you really feel that you are less worthy than anyone else you know?

WHAT NEEDS DO YOU HAVE THAT ARE NOT BEING MET? Your need to experience security is not being fulfilled. This lack may or may not originate from your mate. If your mate is saying or doing things to purposely generate insecurity, you have an entirely different situation than if your feelings of insecurity are the result of past-life subconscious programming. *(If you are not aware of the cause of your insecurity, use the "Back to the Cause" regression technique in Section I.)* Regardless of the cause, you must resolve the conflict within yourself, without expectations of change on the part of your mate.

WHAT ARE YOU DOING THAT CREATES DISHARMONY? Maybe you question your mate about everything he does, or where he is at every moment. Maybe your fears result in stress, which you express as unjustified anger toward him.

WHAT IMMEDIATE ACTIONS CAN YOU TAKE TO CREATE MORE HARMONY? You might stop questioning your mate about his every action . . . or you may need to stop expressing anger. I am not encouraging psychological dissociation, which is a defense mechanism to avoid reality. If you stopped expressing your anger, you would be repressing your real feelings, and in the long term, repression never works. But behavioral changes, based upon greater awareness and logic, will quickly lead to a change in attitude. Once your attitude changes, you'll no longer be repressing your feelings. As your life becomes more harmonious, you'll be encouraged to act even more harmoniously in the future.

If you want your life to get better, you have to do something! Although you may be fearful, with no idea how or even if it will work, you must have the courage to act anyway. The single factor common to all problems—truly, the origin of all problems—is fear. So fear is the place to begin our processing.

FEAR PROCESS

(You may want to record this entire process and explore your reactions in an altered state of consciousness. If so, begin with the induction, then record the

statements and leave an appropriate pause after each question. Trust the very first impressions that form— thoughts, feelings or visualizations—just as in receiving psychically or in past-life regression. Allow them to flow and simply observe where they go.)

The first fear-based emotion is *blame.* If you blame others for your fate or circumstances, you are playing the part of a victim. It is easier to do this than to take responsibility for your life. Blame is incompatible with the concepts of reincarnation and karma, for if everything is karmic, you needed the experience as an opportunity for learning. It is also important to realize that whenever you blame anyone for anything, you're expressing self-pity. So, now, ask yourself the five questions in regard to blame: What is the real fear? *(Pause.)* Is this fear valid? *(Pause.)* What needs do you have that are not being met? *(Pause.)* What are you doing that creates disharmony? *(Pause.)* What immediate actions can you take to create more harmony? *(Pause.)*

The next fear-based emotion is the *need to control.* Whom do you attempt to control? Your mate? Your kids? Your friends? To control means to manipulate, and manipulation is disharmonious, not only for those you manipulate but also for you, because it sets up negative interactions that are extremely destructive. There are eight primary manipulative ploys that people use on others. First is *guilt,* which is always used to hurt or control. Second is *anger*—this is especially effective against those unnerved by openly aggressive behavior. Third is *criticism.* The manipulator finds something wrong with the other person's thinking or behavior and uses criticism to upset his mental balance and make him feel insecure. Fourth is *obligation;* this is often introduced in the form of an unspoken agreement. In other words, "If I do this for you, you'll have to do this for me." Fifth is *withhold-*

ing, primarily used in close relationships. Sixth is *helplessness*—the manipulator claims that he can't do what he needs to do unless you do what he wants you to do. Seventh is *teasing,* apparently loving and affectionate, but the teaser is always making a hidden statement. Eighth is *questioning;* the manipulator asks questions to which he already knows the answers, usually to make the other person admit that they were wrong or in error.

All right, in regard to the need to control: Whom do you attempt to control or manipulate? *(Pause.)* What is your real fear behind this need to control? *(Pause.)* Is this fear valid? *(Pause.)* What needs do you have that aren't being met that cause you to feel this need to control? *(Pause.)* What actions can you take immediately to create more harmony? *(Pause.)*

The next fear-based emotion is *anxiety,* which in turn creates *tension.* Anxiety is a feeling of dread and apprehension about the future that has no specific cause. Tension results when anxiety is accompanied by feelings of muscular strain. We often hide from anxiety by keeping so busy that there is no time to think about our fears. This is a subconscious strategy to avoid pain, but the anxiety is always there, waiting to emerge as soon as you relax. So, you must either live your life in a constant attempt to avoid anxiety, or you must face your fears and resolve them.

The first processing question is, who or what causes you to become tense or anxious? *(Pause.)* In regard to this tension and anxiety, what is the real fear? *(Pause.)* Is this fear valid? *(Pause.)* How are you acting disharmoniously in response to the tension and anxiety? *(Pause.)* In regard to this, what actions can you take immediately to create more harmony? *(Pause.)*

The next fear-based emotion is *resistance.* Whom or what do you resist? Whom do you desire to be different than they are? Buddha's teachings can be best summarized in his words, "It is your resistance to *what is* that causes your suffering." There are certain things in life that you have the potential to change—if you want them changed badly enough, go ahead and change them. But there are other things that are unchangeable. If you can't tell the difference between mutable and immutable, you will go through life resisting what is. So, it is critical to your well-being that you learn to recognize the areas of your life that can't be changed, so you will stop wasting time and energy on your frustrations and the negative subconscious programming they produce.

The most common area of resistance is wanting other people to be the way you want them to be instead of the way they are. In reality, you can't change another person unless they want to change. You may be in a position to force the change by threatening to leave if they don't comply with your wishes, but that will only cause the other person to repress his real emotions, and that repression will surface in other, possibly more undesirable ways.

We are all free human beings and should be respected for what we are, not for what someone else wants us to be. Of course, there is nothing wrong with trying to influence others. We do this all the time. Nearly everything we say is an attempt to influence others, even if we're only trying to get them to listen to us. What is wrong or disharmonious is to become negative in your resistance. If you are unwilling to accept the other person unless he or she changes, you are probably making a mistake.

Exceptions might be situations of violence or physical abuse, alcoholism, or drug addiction. In such extreme situations, the only way to be responsible to yourself might be to remove yourself from the environment.

But let's get back to the fear processing. Whom or

what do you resist? Whom do you desire to be different than they are? What upsets you because it is the way it is? *(Pause.)* In regard to your resistance, what is the real fear? *(Pause.)* Is this fear valid? *(Pause.)* What needs do you have that are not being met? *(Pause.)* Exactly what do you do to create disharmony? *(Pause.)* What actions can you take to immediately generate more harmony? *(Pause.)*

The next fear-based emotion is *hatred*. Whom do you hate or really dislike? Your ex-mate, your boss, the person in the past who ripped you off? Hatred is not only self-destructive from the perspective of subconscious programming, it is this very programming that will draw what you hate back to you. Hatred is an attempt to separate from the hated person. Karmically, even if you do not draw back the same person, you will draw into your life someone with the same tendencies. And if your hatred isn't balanced in this lifetime, it will have to be dealt with in a future incarnation.

Hatred and strong dislike must also be examined in the light of the Universal Law of Attraction. The law says, "Where your attention goes, your energy flows." You attract what you are and that which you concentrate upon. If you express hatred, you will draw it to you. You always attract the qualities you possess. If you want peace and harmony in your life, you must become peaceful and harmonious.

So, let's explore this fear area. Whom do you hate or really dislike? *(Pause.)* What is the real fear? *(Pause.)* Is this fear valid? *(Pause.)* In regard to this hatred, what needs do you have that are not being met? *(Pause.)* What do you do that creates the disharmony? *(Pause.)* What actions can you take immediately to create more harmony? *(Pause.)*

The next fear-based emotion is *desire for revenge*. Whom would you like to see "get what is coming to them"? All the concepts relating to hatred and strong dislike also apply to the cancerous emotion of revenge. If you seek revenge or would enjoy someone else's suffering, it is time to focus on the individual or group that you hope will experience disharmony. *(Pause.)* What is the real fear? *(Pause.)* Is this fear valid? *(Pause.)* What needs do you have in regard to this situation that are not being met or were not being met at one time? *(Pause.)* What do you do or have you done that creates disharmony in this area? *(Pause.)* What immediate actions can you take to create more harmony? *(Pause.)*

The next fear-based emotion is *anger*. You could not possibly be angry with someone else unless you had expectations related to either approval or control. You expected to attain the other person's approval, or you desired to control his actions or reactions. So, the first question you have to ask yourself is, "Do I have the right to expect other people to be the way I want them to be?" Another way to look at this is, your expectations were in conflict with *what is*. It would be impossible for you to be upset about anything if your expectations were not in conflict with what is. Even if the other person is a complete jerk, that's what is. You expected him to be something other than what he is.

Another way to look at anger is to realize that it arises as a protection against pain. When someone directly or indirectly challenges you or makes you feel bad, your anger is a defense against the pain. To rise above anger, you must understand the futility of expectations and the self-destructive subconscious programming that the anger will produce. From this logical awareness, you can learn to act in your own self-interest, instead of self-destructively.

Let's go back to the anger processing. Who or what causes you to become angry? *(Pause.)* What is the real fear? *(Pause.)* Is this fear valid? *(Pause.)* What needs do you have that are not being met? *(Pause.)* What immediate actions can you take to create more harmony? *(Pause.)*

The next fear-based emotion is *jealousy.* Whom are you jealous of? Your mate or lover? Who or what pushes your jealousy buttons? Jealousy is an emotion that seems justified by a mental position you have adopted. This position is based on your belief that you require someone or something in order to be complete. Your very survival appears to depend on this. In reality you know this is not so; and you know that if jealousy is allowed to manifest itself fully, it drives others away.

Let's process jealousy. Whom or what are you jealous of? *(Pause.)* What is the real fear? *(Pause.)* Is this fear valid? *(Pause.)* In regard to your jealousy, what needs do you have that are not being met? *(Pause.)* What do you do that creates disharmony? *(Pause.)* What immediate actions can you take to create more harmony? *(Pause.)*

The next fear-based emotion is the *need for approval.* Whose approval do you need? If you live for the approval of others, you can never be whoever you really are, because you're afraid it is not good enough to get the approval you feel you need. This concern with what others think will cause you to lose your own identity.

Your primary mistake is believing you need the approval of others. Realize that what others say or do does not affect you; it is only what you think about what they say that affects you. Also remember that people's reactions to you come from their past experiences and conditioning—their narrow view of reality and how things should be. It is their viewpoint and it has nothing to do with you. People live their lives preoccupied with themselves. The way they relate to you is the way they would relate to anyone who represents to them what you represent. Thus, it is foolish to take anything personally, good or bad.

The first processing question about the need for approval is, whose approval do you need? *(Pause.)* In regard to your need of approval, what is the real fear? *(Pause.)* Is the fear valid? *(Pause.)* What needs do you have that are not being met? *(Pause.)* What immediate actions can you take to create more harmony? *(Pause.)*

The next fear-based emotion is *greed*. Greed is the fear of not having enough, a desire for more that fails to recognize the total futility of such a goal. Greed is preparing to live as opposed to living now, in the moment. The Universal Law of Gratitude is the other side of greed. It says, the more you give the more you will receive. The more you assist others, the more you assist yourself. A fearless person is not greedy at all.

Let's process the fear behind greed. What are the primary areas where you express your greed? *(Pause.)* In regard to this greed, what is the real fear? *(Pause.)* Is this fear valid? *(Pause.)* What needs do you have in these areas that are not being met? *(Pause.)* What do you do that creates disharmony? *(Pause.)* What immediate actions can you take to create more harmony in your life? *(Pause.)*

The next fear-based emotion is *inhibition.* What are your primary areas of inhibition? Sex? Meeting new people? Saying what you think or feel? Inhibition is a mental blockage, a fear of behaving in an unconventional manner—the result of being afraid of what other people will think or how they will respond. Much of the above perspective on "need for approval" applies to inhibition, as well.

What are your primary areas of inhibition? *(Pause.)* In regard to your inhibitions, what is the real fear? *(Pause.)* Is this fear valid? *(Pause.)* What needs do you have in the area of inhibition that are not being met? *(Pause.)* What do you do regarding inhibitions that create disharmony? *(Pause.)* What immediate actions can you take to create more harmony? *(Pause.)*

The next fear-based emotion is *frustration*. Who or what frustrates you? Frustration is the negative result of your expectations. The individual who attains self-actualization learns to live without expectations, thus he can't possibly experience frustration.

When you have expectations about something and your experience doesn't live up to your expectations, you'll be disappointed or unable to enjoy the experience for what it is. We experience the most disappointments in dealing with other people. Whenever you expect someone else to be the way you want him to be, you're headed for conflict.

Let's process your expectations. Who or what frustrates you? Is there a pattern to your frustration? *(Pause.)* What is the real fear behind the frustration? *(Pause.)* Is the fear valid? *(Pause.)* In regard to the frustration, what needs do you have that are not being met? *(Pause.)* What do you do that creates disharmony in your life? *(Pause.)* What immediate actions can you take to create harmony? *(Pause.)*

The next fear-based emotion is *envy*. Whom or what do you envy? If your envy is a response to someone who has more possessions, or is healthier, or has a more beautiful body, or enjoys more money, prestige, or career success or satisfaction, then your real problem is comparison. We are all raised from childhood to compare, but if you stop comparing, envy will disappear.

Let's process your envy. Whom or what do you envy? *(Pause.)* What is the real fear behind this envy? *(Pause.)* Is this fear valid? *(Pause.)* What needs do you have in regard to this envy that are not being met? *(Pause.)* What do you do that creates disharmony? *(Pause.)* What immediate actions can you take to create more harmony? *(Pause.)*

The next fear-based emotion is *possessiveness*. Whom or what do you feel possessive about—your mate or lover, your friend, your home, your car? This is a form of insanity that is self-perpetuating. The possessor needs to possess more things, more money, more power, more people—more of everything.

If the need is to possess a person, the object of that need will always experience a dichotomy. He or she will feel complimented at being so highly valued but will also want to be free. Often, an overwhelming desire to possess can be traced to feelings of deprivation or loss, even though the "lost" object may not be identifiable. So the response is to hold on all the tighter to ensure that nothing else slips away.

Let's process your possessiveness. Whom or what do you feel possessive about? *(Pause.)* What is the real fear behind this possessiveness? *(Pause.)* Is this fear valid? *(Pause.)* In regard to your possessiveness, what needs do you have that are not being met? *(Pause.)* What do you do that creates disharmony? *(Pause.)* What immediate actions can you take to create more harmony? *(Pause.)*

The next fear-based emotion is *insecurity*. Life is insecure! Love is insecure! You are always moving from the known to the unknown. But no matter how much you resist this awareness, the situation will not change. Even if you were to attain total security, you would soon become bored. The real problem lies in how you view the issue of insecurity.

It is the unknown that makes life exciting, and it is insecurity that allows you to experience your *aliveness* —the stimulation that makes life worth living. Look back on the times you really knew you were alive— the rush, the titillation, the thrill. You may have experienced aliveness on a roller coaster ride, or during the early stages of a romance. Maybe it was while fighting in a war, or when you started your own business and didn't know whether you'd succeed or not. Insecurity is not knowing how life is going to turn out. But if you knew how it would turn out, life would become dull and mundane.

Let's process your insecurity. Who or what causes you to feel insecure? *(Pause.)* What is the real fear behind the insecurity? *(Pause.)* Is this fear valid? *(Pause.)* In regard to this insecurity, what do you do that creates disharmony in your life? *(Pause.)* What immediate actions can you take to create more harmony? *(Pause.)*

The next fear-based emotion is *guilt*. Guilt is an attempt to make right in the present something you did or thought you were doing wrong. Guilt always inhibits you, and causes you to monitor your thoughts too much. Each time you think about it you generate more negative subconscious programming, so guilt is obviously self-destructive. There are ten primary areas where we tend to feel guilty, and we'll explore them one at a time.

1. *Religious guilt:* For centuries, religions have used guilt as their primary tool for exploiting and controlling people. By creating guilt within you, the church makes you feel bad about yourself and dependent on the priest for absolution. Don't believe it. Do you feel any religious guilt? *(Pause.)* What is the real fear? *(Pause.)* Is this fear valid? *(Pause.)* In regard to this guilt, what needs do you have that aren't being met? *(Pause.)* In regard to this guilt, what do you do that creates disharmony? *(Pause.)* What can you do to create more harmony?

2. *Parental Guilt:* Do you feel guilty in any way toward your parents? *(Ask the five questions.)*

3. *Sexual Infidelity Guilt:* Have you cheated in a sexual relationship and now feel guilty about it? *(Ask the five questions.)*

4. *Sexual Practice Guilt:* Is there something you do

or have done sexually that causes you to feel guilty? *(Ask the five questions.)*

5. *Someone You Hurt in the Past Guilt:* Is there anyone in the past you hurt, or cheated, or manipulated, or took advantage of that still causes you to feel guilt in the present? *(Ask the five questions.)*

6. *Someone You Neglected Guilt:* Is there someone in your past you neglected that causes guilt in the present? *(Ask the five questions.)*

7. *Someone You Could Have Helped But Turned Your Back On Guilt:* Is there someone in your past you could have helped but didn't, and it is still bothering you? *(Ask the five questions.)*

8. *Philosophical Guilt:* Is there an area where you have a philosophical or ethical belief not reflected in your actions that is causing you guilt? For example, if you have an avowed commitment to animal rights and vegetarianism but you occasionally sneak a hamburger or wear animal hide boots, you may experience guilt. *(Ask the five questions.)*

9. *An Act of Cowardice Guilt:* Do you feel guilty about an act of cowardice in your past? *(Ask the five questions.)*

10. *An Act of Cruelty Guilt:* Is there an instance of cruelty in your past that still bothers you? *(Ask the five questions.)*

Our feelings of guilt may be the result of a current situation or one that is long standing. Let's explore potential guilt feelings in these three areas: *current, long-standing guilt,* and *philosophical guilt.*

For example, *current guilt* might be a reaction to not spending enough quality time with your children; *long-standing guilt* might develop because you left your ex-husband; and *philosophical guilt* might result from failing to share your good fortune by tithing ten percent to your church.

Since no one can change the past, long-standing

guilt is always inappropriate. You can't undo what is done, and to dwell on it destroys the present and the future. But current guilt and philosophical guilt you can do something about . . . if you choose to. In choosing guilt, you choose to see yourself as bad. You want to gain self-acceptance and you can't do this when you feel you are bad, *unless you make yourself feel guilty*. It's a stupid, internal, debit-and-credit system. Once you've felt guilty long enough it balances or justifies your actions so you can feel okay with yourself. But usually, you just do the same thing all over again. It is a never-ending spiral, unless you decide to end it.

Meditate on the three factors and your willingness to give up guilt. *(Long pause.)*

(Awaken script—end of altered-state process.)

I've covered some of the major fear-based emotions in this chapter, though there are many more that we do not have the space to discuss. However, you can see from the examples I've included how to work on processing any of the fear-based emotions.

One last subject I wish to cover in this chapter is stress. Though not an emotion itself, stress can develop if we are exposed enough to any of the fear-based emotions. Although not all stress is bad, too much is usually destructive to your mental and physical well-being. You don't want to fight or resist stress—that will only make it worse. Instead, welcome it, accept it, and flow with it. I suggest that you convert your stress to creative energy; use it to fuel positive activities, such as taking a walk, working on a hobby, or completing some other project. Once you totally accept the stress, it will begin to disappear. Developing mental detachment will help you to do this.

CHAPTER

11

Handling Fear

Fear is responsible for every disturbance, large or small, international or interpersonal. Although I've been showing you how to process the many aspects of fear, there is really only one fear—the fear of being unable to cope. All fears grow from this one. Whether it is rejection you fear, or a person, animal, or inanimate object; whether you're greedy, possessive, or anxious; or even if you're simply afraid of aging or death, what you really fear is being unable to cope with the fearful situation, should you encounter it.

Maybe you don't like your mate and want to change him. You criticize, avoid, and reject him, but you must see that the fear is within you. And you must act to learn to cope with your mate. If you will make immediate changes in your behavior, they can lead to a change in attitude, in turn leading to the fulfillment of your needs. Change begins with action!

Maybe your neighbor is a constant talker. You hope she doesn't come over because she wastes your time—you get nothing done, she intrudes on your privacy, and you don't particularly like her; you tolerate her intrusions because you don't want to hurt her feelings.

You wear an "I'm a nice person" mask because if you make her feel bad then you'll feel guilty and you want to avoid this. It's fear, fear, fear! But the moment you are direct and honest with her, you will no longer dread her approach. Say to her, "In the future, I want you to call me before you come over. I need more privacy. I hope you can understand." All you have done is assert your basic human rights. By taking off your mask and coping with your neighbor, you *rise above the effects of fear.*

By doing this, you *transform* the fear, altering your viewpoint—how you perceive the realities of your life and your relationship to them. The realities seldom change.

There are obviously positive and negative sides to fear. For example, fear might keep you awake when falling asleep would be disastrous. But if fear keeps you from making a beneficial growth choice, you need to explore the fear. A joyful, fulfilling life entails risks. And encountering fear is part of the risk-taking process. Accept it and act anyway. That's what courage is all about: *to act despite your fear.*

Fear too often paralyzes people. Refusing to act, they close down and begin to avoid life. The end result? Life becomes dull and boring. And, when life becomes too mundane, you will do something to create excitement—even if it is self-destructive. An extramarital affair would spice up your life. A good fight with your mate will get your blood pumping and let you know you're still alive. Dangerous driving could give you a thrill. There is always an endless list of self-destructive or thrill-seeking actions that will add the missing elements necessary to make life interesting again.

Others whose lives are dull and boring exercise great self-control. Their lives are so safe and so dull that even though they have not indulged in self-destructive activities, the dark side of the mind has to create something to make life more exciting. This is the way human beings work. Your mind cannot tolerate a boring, ho-hum existence forever, and if you exert too much self-control for too long, your mind will find other ways to make life interesting again. How about an illness to give you something to talk about? Or a tragic accident to make life meaningful again?

The answer is not to close down, avoiding circumstances because of your fears. You must not allow fear-based emotions to keep you from making growth choices—*you must act anyway!* You must embrace your fears and experience them fully. *When you fully experience your fear, you will rise above it!* Then you can throw off your limitations and begin to live up to your potential.

All your fears relate back to your past programming, or viewpoint. It is your viewpoint that causes you to feel anxious about the future, but you can change your viewpoint by acting in the face of fear. Reality exists as that which you experience. The way you experience life is a result of how you choose to view what happens to you.

By altering your perspective on the situation—your viewpoint—you can eliminate the effects of a problem. And, if you are no longer affected by a problem, you no longer have a problem, even though nothing about the situation may have changed.

As an example, let's say your husband is a male chauvinist. This upsets you, but rather than acting out hostility or anger, you decide to change your viewpoint. You realize you can't change him, but you can change yourself. Your choices are clear: 1. You can continue to be upset about the way he is, which is ridiculous because he is never going to change. All you are doing is hurting yourself. 2. You can leave, but male chauvinist or not, you love him so this is not a consideration. 3. You can accept him the way he is. Once you stop resisting what he is, you are no longer affected by the problem, so you don't have a problem, although nothing about the situation has changed except your viewpoint.

Another aspect of fear is that no one worries about what has happened in the past. Even if you experience guilt about past events, you aren't worried about the past, only about your continuing reaction to what happened in the past.

Fear is sustained by your thoughts and memories about the past situation. When you recall your fears, you are filled with anxiety. You're afraid of public opinion. You're afraid of losing your job. You're afraid your wife might run off. You're afraid of being lonely. You're afraid of not being loved. You're afraid of dying. You're afraid of rattlesnakes. As I stated before, all fears are, in essence, one fear—the fear of what will happen in the future and your ability or inability to cope with it. Let's say you are walking in the woods and you're afraid you'll come across a rattlesnake—the fear of a future event. Let's suppose you do encounter a rattlesnake—then you're afraid he is going to bite you—again, in a future moment. Then he does bite you and you're afraid of dying—in the future.

Fears always relate to a future event; so, you must learn to live in the present, the now. You will start to do this once you understand your fears and choose to be uncomfortable by acting instead of avoiding the situations that make you feel afraid.

What else can you do to let go of fear? Uncovering the original cause of the fear is often very helpful in assisting you to let go of the undesirable effects. Use the Back to the Cause regression script in Chapter 4. Reprogramming with self-hypnosis is a very powerful tool for letting go of fear, although it often must be done for many weeks or months to be effective. This technique is discussed in Section III.

CONSCIOUS DETACHMENT

Conscious detachment is the enlightened approach to releasing fear-based emotions. There are two states of mind: *attached mind* and *detached mind*. Most of the world experiences attached mind, so their outlook changes from positive to negative as outside conditions change. They experience extreme fluctuation from happiness and joy, through neutral, into anger, hostility, depression, and other fear-based emotions.

Examples of attached mind: 1. You are enjoying a relaxing afternoon with your mate until he says something to irritate you. Your response is anger. 2. Everything is going along very well until someone runs into your car. You feel moody and upset. 3. You are proud of the presentation you made at work, until someone whose opinion you respect criticizes your effort. You become quite depressed.

Detached mind means your state of mind fluctuates only from positive to neutral as outside conditions change. You accept all the warmth, joy, and happiness that life has to offer while detaching from the negativity by allowing it to flow through you without affecting you.

Examples of detached mind: 1. You are having a relaxing afternoon with your mate until she says something negative. Your response is neutral. You realize that it isn't what someone says to you that affects you, it is only what *you think* about what they say that affects you. It's what you add to it. You're also aware that her response is only an expression of her past programming, so to take it personally is foolish.

2. Everything is going well until someone runs into your car. You certainly aren't happy about it, yet you accept what is because you know all the resistance in the world won't change it. So why bother? Why complicate or program your life negatively? You simply do what you have to do to resolve the situation with a minimum of inconvenience. 3. You are proud of your presentation at work. When someone whose opinion you respect criticizes your efforts, you are unaffected by the remark. You know your critic is expressing his viewpoint, which may have nothing to do with the facts. You are detached from the need to be right.

To develop conscious detachment means to detach from the negativity in your life. It does not mean having no feelings or sensations, such as hunger or pain. It is not a matter of ignoring faults or mistakes. You simply stop judging and labeling what happens to you. I'm talking about being totally involved in your life and enjoying everything there is to enjoy, while detaching from the negativity. By eliminating the negativity, you have more time and room for love and warm interaction. When you cease to be concerned with negativity, you'll be more likely to enter into whatever you do without holding anything back, free to be entirely one with circumstances.

Obviously, you can't develop a detached mind overnight, but by keeping it before you as a goal you can eventually transcend fear. In fact, it's one element in the ultimate combination to end suffering and attain peace of mind: an understanding of how your viewpoint creates your reality, the acceptance of unalterable realities (what is), an awareness of the self-responsibility of karma, and the concept of conscious detachment.

CHAPTER

12

Masks and Patterns

You won't recognize the wisdom of detachment or the truth of what is because you are more intelligent than others, but because of your character, which is based on self-actualized awareness. What's your character based on? *Courage!* To embrace the truth means to reject the commands of power . . . the demands of society and public opinion. To embrace the truth means you no longer tolerate helplessness. You demand the freedom that is your birthright—the freedom to become all you are capable of being.

Society seeks to mold its members into "ladies" and "gentlemen," or, in other words, phonies and hypocrites. These are people wearing the mask of "proper" attire and etiquette. Ladies and gentlemen say and do the "right" thing; they are role-playing personas, very conventional and cast from the same mold—mediocrity! They are so concerned with what other people think that they lose their own identity.

Ladies and gentlemen are perfect examples of repression. They avoid reality, hiding behind social masks, while their fear-based frustrations, anger, and desires fuel the dark fantasies that program their subconscious minds.

It doesn't have to be this way. Ladies and gentlemen can learn to remove their masks and become the men and women they really are beneath the disguise. Of course, there are dangers involved in being real. Some people may turn against you when you discard the familiar mask. What that means is that the relationship is based on your willingness to allow them to manipulate you into being what they want you to be. Do you need any relationship that badly?

The only reason to wear a mask is to keep out pain. The primary problem is that if your mask deflects pain, it will also keep out your full potential for joy and destroy your sense of aliveness. To attain enlightenment you must come to know your true self— which is not easy to do. Your masks keep even you from knowing who you are. The true self cannot be found until your false self is renounced—which means letting go of your masks. When you can function as your true self, you can experience loving yourself for the first time, and then you will be in a position to love others unconditionally.

Human potential trainers know there are three ways to bring about change in a human being. 1. You can *add* something—people, things, environment, awareness, or challenge. 2. You can *subtract* something— people, things, environment, programming, or challenge. 3. You can get the person *to be himself*— transcendental change—when an individual discards his fears and expands himself. So, to break the chains of illusion, you must come to know what you really are, even if it seems very ugly to you. Acceptance of reality is the first step to wisdom—you can't change what you don't recognize.

It is necessary to explore your own masks, whatever they may be. I won't advise that you throw away all your masks, but you do need to understand the reason you wear each one and explore the price you pay for wearing it. Masks are repression and repression is fear. Repression will manifest itself in one way or another. One person represses himself and develops an ulcer. Another has a skin rash or allergies. Someone else takes it out on his mate or kicks the family dog. Some people repress their real emotions for years—until they get cancer. There is always a price.

Through the self-examination process, you may also discover that the reason you wear the mask is no longer valid, but is generated by an old fear that does not relate to your life now.

MASK EXAMPLES

The mask of indifference is quite common. The wearer pretends something doesn't matter or pretends he doesn't care about it. The dumb mask is usually worn more by women than by men. She pretends to be dumb to avoid getting the point or to avoid facing a reality she doesn't want to face. The talkative mask is worn by the person who can't keep quiet because he is nervous or insecure about something, even if it's just the silence when he stops. He thinks if he's not talking ninety miles per hour others will feel ignored.

The joker mask is worn by the man or woman who constantly interjects witty remarks into every conversation. They may need excessive attention because of underlying insecurity, or they wear the mask to avoid things, whether simple issues or major confrontations, as a way to deflect real contact or intimacy. The quiet mask is worn by people who sit back and remain silent because they are afraid they might expose themselves by saying something stupid, or because they feel superior.

The workaholic mask is usually worn to avoid something—undesired social contact, intimate interactions at home—or it may be a greed mask. Greed masks offer a rationalization for working extra hours due to financial need, but often the individual has created this need to justify the work. The "poor little me" mask is the favorite of problem-oriented people. A life full of problems gives the wearer something to talk about. Others pretend to feel sorry for them and they get attention.

The mask I've most often encountered in New Agers is the "extra nice mask." These people think they should be extra nice to everyone because that's the spiritual way. In reality, though, there is fear lurking behind the mask. Maybe Ms. Extra Nice gets off on being needed, so it is a power play. She gets to feel superior—"I'm always there when she needs me!" And the ego gets pumped. But more often than not people are extra nice because they are afraid that they won't be liked if they are themselves. So they attempt to make everyone feel good, valued, and desired. They may also be afraid that if others feel uncomfortable, they will, too.

Mr. and Mrs. Extra Nice are usually overpowered by people in a very short time. Then they need to get away and hide to recuperate. Their mask gets so heavy that they have to escape and regain the strength to hold it up again, yet if they were just direct and honest in their communications, they would find it takes no extra energy at all and they would lose the need to hide.

The secret to throwing away your masks is simply to be who you really are underneath: to say what you honestly think and feel, and to assert your basic human rights. A process to assist you identify your masks follows. If you choose to record the process for exploration in an altered state, I suggest that you leave lengthy pauses after each question, or that you go into trance with your index finger on the pause button so you can shut off the tape player and take as much time as necessary to explore each question.

The Masks Process will pose a series of questions to help you explore each of these false identities. The five questions are:

1. What are the supposed benefits of wearing this mask?
2. The mask is repression, so what is the real fear?
3. How would I (they) respond if I (they) were being direct and honest?
4. What is the price of wearing the mask?
5. What is the worst that would happen if I took off this mask?

Masks Process

(Induction first) And I am now relaxed and at ease and peacefully centered, in balance and harmony. It is time to explore the concept of masks. First, pick a person in my life who irritates me. *(Pause.)* What kind of a mask does the person wear? *(Pause.)* What kind of a mask do I wear when responding to the person? *(Pause.)* (The five questions.) What are the supposed benefits of wearing this mask? *(Pause.)* The mask is repression, so what is the real fear? *(Pause.)* How would I respond if I were direct and honest? *(Pause.)* What is the price of wearing this mask? *(Pause.)* What is the worst that would happen if I took off this mask? *(Pause.)*

Pick a person I avoid seeing. *(Pause.)* What kind of mask does this person wear? *(Pause.)* What kind of mask do I wear when I see him? *(Pause.)* *(Ask the five questions.)*

Pick a person I have a hard time saying "no" to. *(Pause.)* What kind of a mask does the person wear? *(Pause.)* What kind of mask do I wear in his presence? *(Pause.)* (Ask the five questions.)

Pick a friend who wears a mask. *(Pause.)* What kind of mask does the friend wear? *(Pause.)* What kind of mask do I wear when responding to him? *(Pause.) (Ask the five questions.)*

See my mate or the person closest to me wearing one of his masks. *(Pause.)* When he wears it, what kind of mask do I wear in response? *(Pause.) (Ask the five questions.)*

See my boss or a fellow employee and examine his mask and the one I use to deal with him. *(Pause.) (Ask the five questions.)*

Recall meeting someone for the first time and explore the mask I was wearing. *(Pause.) (Ask the five questions.)*

Recall meeting a potential lover for the first time and explore the mask I was wearing. *(Pause.) (Ask the five questions.)*

What is my primary mask, if I were to choose just one? *(Pause.) (Ask the five questions.)*

Explore a secondary mask I often wear. *(Pause.) (Ask the five questions.)*

What do I need to know that I don't know that would allow me to take off my masks? *(Pause.)*

(Awaken.)

The next step in this exploration is to investigate patterned behaviors. It's time to look back over your life and become aware of your primary life patterns.

Patterned Behavior Process

(Induction first.) I am now relaxed and at ease and peacefully centered. I feel in balance and in harmony.

And it is time to explore my primary life patterns, beginning with my primary relationships with a mate or lover. Are there patterns in my relationships that continue to emerge? *(Pause.) (Examples: 1. The moment your mate is critical of you, you close down and refuse to communicate. 2. When you are finally assured of your mate's love and dedication to the relationship, you become bored. 3. Your partner begins to manipulate to get what he wants and you begin to resist the manipulation with increasing intensity. 4. You have a history of affairs. 5. You have a history of using work to deflect intimacy. 6. You have a history of neglecting the relationship in favor of involvement with friends.)* There are thousands of patterns in relationships. Examine yours and any related masks.

Now it is time to explore any behavior patterns in my sex life. There may be several and I need to explore those that are not working for me. Also, I'll examine any masks I might be wearing and the fears behind the masks. *(Pause.)*

Explore any patterns in my relationships with my children and family members. Also examine any related masks and the fears behind the masks. *(Pause.)*

Explore any behavior patterns that relate to my career or the primary way I spend my time. Also examine any masks and the fears behind the masks. *(Pause.) (Examples: 1. You only allow yourself to attain a limited level of success before you do something to cancel it out. 2. You allow frustrations to build up until you are "mad" enough to force a change.)*

Explore any patterns like obsessive behaviors or undesirable habits you may have developed. Look carefully at any masks and the fears behind the masks. *(Pause.)*

Explore any patterns of behavior related to my spirituality. Examine any masks and the fears behind the masks. *(Pause.)*

Explore any patterns of behavior regarding my interests or hobbies. Examine any masks and the fears behind the masks. *(Pause.)*

The last area of exploration is service to others and to the planet. Study my attitudes and any patterns of behavior. *(Pause.)*

What patterns have I discovered that do not work for me and what can I do about them? *(Long pause.)* *(Awaken.)*

I hope you have discovered that every negative behavior pattern is based on fear. And it is these fears that keep you from expressing unconditional love. To change these behavior patterns, you need to let go of the fear and break the chains of illusion by expanding your awareness.

Each step on the path to enlightenment takes you deeper into your center. When you are finally there, deep within your true self, you make contact with the collective unconscious, the awareness of the totality. The collective unconscious is the God portion of your totality. Those who accept the freedom that comes with this kind of thinking also accept four basic assumptions: 1. All is one: The external world and consciousness are one and the same. 2. Man is a Divine being: We are all part of God, so we are God. 3. The purpose of life is to help us evolve spiritually (through reincarnation and karma). 4. Self-actualization is possible: Awareness of the true self within leads to mastery of your own reality.

CHAPTER

13

Expectations and Repression

EXPECTATIONS

Expectations, your own or those of others, never work. They are a major kind of illusion—preconceived ideas about how someone or something is going to be. And when the actuality doesn't live up to your expectations, you are disappointed and cannot enjoy the person or situation for what it is.

Expectations simply don't work! An example: You have expectations about how wonderful it will be when you finally get your dream house in the suburbs. When you actually acquire the longed-for dream house, the reality is that it doesn't measure up—for one reason or another—to your fantasy. So now you can't even enjoy the house for what it is because your expectations have ruined it for you.

Another example might be your expectations about a romantic encounter. When the romance didn't live up to the fantasy, you probably didn't even enjoy the relationship for what it did offer. The same might apply to a vacation. You dream of an idyllic cruise to Hawaii, meeting wonderful creative people on the ship, swimming at remote white sand beaches, and enjoying the exciting night life. But once on board, you discover that 99 percent of the passengers belong to the Retired Farmer's League of Davenport, Iowa. Then, when you get to Hawaii, it is the rainy season and too cool to enjoy the beaches. The exciting night life in the area consists of two bands playing country music for the Farmer's League. Since reality didn't match your expectations, you become depressed. That's your choice. The alternative is to forget about expectations and simply enjoy each aspect of your vacation for what it is and what you can make of it under the circumstances. Living in the moment, without expectations, guarantees that you won't be disappointed.

What about the expectations of others? If you attempt to live up to them, they will cripple and paralyze you. Expectations are your enemy. You may choose to accept some responsibilities toward your mate, your children or your career, but aside from that, the expectations of others—your friends, associates, and probably many family members—will control you because they will activate your fears about what other people think. *It doesn't matter what they think.* If they are not going to like you unless you meet their expectations, you're nothing but a puppet. You don't need them. There are plenty of people in the world who will gladly accept you just the way you are. All you need is the courage to live more dangerously, to cut loose from the past and embrace new challenges in your life.

Enlightenment means discovering and living from your true self . . . your true nature. This expanded awareness includes understanding the true nature of

Judeo-Christian reality, which is always based on a moral urgency to be "right." This perspective permeates our lives. It views the world as a struggle of good against bad, spiritual against unspiritual, moral against immoral. It uses God to enslave people's minds, and in the name of the church it has exploited humanity for centuries.

The result for most of us is anxiety, frustration, and repression. We are conditioned from childhood to respond to guilt. But if we want to attain true freedom from the self, we have to change the way we view reality. To break the chains of illusion you must accept that what you think is more important than what other people think.

There is no such thing as right and wrong, ethical and unethical, moral and immoral. A group of people agree on terminology, and maybe they agree to call a particular action ethical. But calling it ethical doesn't make it ethical—it only means that's what one group has decided to call it. It doesn't change what actually is. Some languages have no word for rape and it is not even a concept in the areas where that language is spoken; men assume they have the right to take women by force at their whim. On some Polynesian islands, open sexuality is moral and beautiful. So you can see that right, wrong, moral, and immoral are all concepts that change with the times, and in fact exist only because a certain group or the majority of people agrees on them.

To live in a particular society, you must be willing to accept the consequences of your actions in regard to the laws of the society. Yet most of the time there is no legal issue involved when our actions are not in keeping with the opinions of others. It is ill-advised for you to repress who and what you really are because of what other people think.

REPRESSION

Repression is a problem we all share to different degrees, and it is a big one. It can be more harmful in the long run than indulgence, because you eventually get tired of whatever you indulge in. The poet William Blake said, "The road to excess leads to the palace of wisdom." But repression never goes away. It simply lies deep within you, waiting for an opportunity to assert itself.

Most people in this country don't understand the teachings of Bhagwan Shree Rajneesh. They get stuck on some of his more radical ideas, such as his encouragement of open sexuality. But I've always believed Rajneesh is far wiser than most gurus. He knows that by encouraging the expression of sexuality, his followers will quickly move past their sexual obsessions.

When you repress yourself, you ultimately end up feeling that you haven't lived; then the repression becomes a mental problem. Rajneesh says, "If you feel the need to express your sexuality, it is God-given energy. That means there is something to be learned through the experience." I agree, as long as your sexual activities are not hurting yourself or anyone else in any way.

Esoteric metaphysics teaches that when you repress what you really are and what you really desire to do, it generates a vibrational energy within your soul that will have to be expressed—if not in this life, then in the next. Because repression is based on fear, it will always be disharmonious to your soul goal of expanding awareness.

In a seminar, a middle-age man once explained to me that he had always wanted to experience sex with a man but repressed his desire.

"Why do you repress this desire?" I asked.

"Oh, I think it's wrong. And maybe I'm also afraid I

might like it. I might make myself crazier than I already am," he replied with a nervous laugh.

I asked him about his current relationships, and he explained that he was divorced, and dated several different women. He enjoyed sex with them, but admitted to frequent fantasies of making love to a man.

I related the "right and wrong, moral and immoral" concept, and explained that from my perspective as a past-life therapist and human potential trainer, homosexuality is simply a life-style choice—a karmic decision based on the particular restrictions and growth opportunities it offers. You might be heterosexual, bisexual, homosexual, or celibate—none of these options have anything to do with morality. Instead, you select the one that best fits your karmic configuration, the one that will be of most value in rounding out your awareness, and especially, the one that best allows you the opportunity to let go of fear and express unconditional love.

A couple of months after the seminar, this man wrote to me saying, "Thank you a million times over. After the seminar, I found the courage to have an affair with a man. I saw him on many occasions for about four weeks. The experience was beautiful, but I learned that I really prefer to be with women. Now I feel I can make the space in my life for another full-time relationship with the right woman."

It was gratifying to get his letter, but it would have been just as gratifying if he had discovered he was gay and had gone on to establish a different life-style. Either way, he removed a mask of repression and let go of fear. From the perspective of reincarnation, if he had repressed his desire for the homosexual experience he would have generated a vibrational energy within his soul that would eventually have demanded expression—if not in this life then in the next, or in the one after that. This idea scares people. They know what they are repressing, but are unwilling to face and explore the fear.

Janet, a female seminar participant in her late thirties, once explained that she was repressing her feelings about her career. "I'm an advertising agency copywriter, and I'm burned out," she said, making gestures of futility. "I fake it. I'm good enough to write the drivel they want without much effort. I pretend to be the same person I've always been, but every week it gets harder. I watch the clock, hoping the work day will end. I count the minutes to Friday and spend half the weekend dreading Monday."

"What is the fear behind the repression, Janet?" I asked.

"That I need the high-paying salary," she replied.

"Is the fear of needing the high-paying salary valid?" I asked.

"If I want to maintain my life-style."

"What is the price you're paying as a result of your repression?" I continued.

"I don't know," she replied, and stared at the floor thinking about it. "Maybe sleep! I seem to need ten or eleven hours of sleep. Maybe I'm hiding behind sleep. I know my headaches have increased. Rarely do I wake up without a splitting headache and a sense of depression."

"If you were honest and direct, what would you say to your employer?" I asked.

"I quit, because I can't stand to write another damn line of advertising copy!" she said, and laughed.

"Can you predict the probable outcome of that?" I asked.

"I'd obviously have to get another job, doing something else," she said wistfully.

"How would you feel about that?"

"Good, actually. But I doubt that I could make

anywhere near as much money. I'd have to cut back on my life-style."

"And stop hiding behind sleep, waking up with headaches, hating your work, and dreading Mondays," I teased. "Sounds like a good trade-off to me."

"It sounds good to me, too!" she said, suddenly decisive as she placed her hands on her hips. "And then maybe I'd have the energy to write the book I want to write. It's an important book and it could support what I'd really love to do—public speaking." The seminar audience applauded.

Let's do a repression process. If you decide to participate in the ideal way, in an altered state of consciousness, leave long pauses after each major question, or go into trance with your finger on the pause button. In addition to the primary questions, ask yourself the following:

1. What is the real fear behind this repression?
2. Is this fear valid?
3. What is the price I am paying for this repression?
4. What would I do or say if I were honest and direct?
5. If I express my true feelings, the probable outcome will be . . .
6. How would that change my life and how do I feel about it?

Repression Process

(Do the induction first. Remember to trust the very first impressions that form as thoughts, feelings, or visualizations. Allow them to flow and simply observe where they go.) And I am now relaxed and at ease and peacefully centered . . . in balance and harmony. And

it is time to explore any repression I am currently experiencing. In my primary relationship, is there any area in which I am repressing what I really am? *(The question doesn't relate to sex at this time. Explore your day-to-day relationship with your mate or lover.)* Is there any area of my relationship in which I am holding back and not saying what I really want to say, or doing what I really want to do? *(Pause.)* What is the real fear? *(Pause.)* Is this fear valid? *(Pause.)* What is the price I am paying for this repression? *(Pause.)* What would I say or do if I were honest and direct? *(Pause.)* If I express my true feelings, the probable outcome will be . . . *(Pause.)* How would that change my life and how do I feel about it? *(Pause.)*

Let's explore my sex life. *(When you repress sexually, you become angry. The more sex is repressed, the more angry and violent people become. Those who direct armies know this, so the soldier who has no opportunity to experience sex channels his energy and anger into the next battle.)* Am I repressing my sexuality in any way? *(Pause.) (Ask the six questions.)*

Am I repressing feelings about other people in my life—my children, parents, in-laws, relatives, friends, or business associates? *(Pause.) (Ask the six questions.)*

Am I repressing emotions in regard to my career, or the primary way I spend my time? *(Pause.) (Ask the six questions.) (Awaken.)*

Do you understand that repression and masks are really the same thing—just another way of viewing the fears in your life? In my seminars, people will often avoid looking behind their masks, but they can't hide from themselves when the fear is labeled "repression."

CHAPTER

14

Aliveness and Challenge

Enlightenment is dependent upon your attainment of freedom *of* the self and *from* the self. But when you allow society and your fears to mold you, you are giving away your freedom and succumbing to negativity. All too often, you trade your aliveness for security and survival . . . and you close down and burn out. From about the age of thirty on, people begin to burn out and run on the momentum they had generated up to that time.

No matter what you do for a living, it eventually becomes boring. Maybe you enjoyed your work at one time, but with the daily grind to make payments and fulfill your obligations it has become drudgery. And frequently, for many people, it follows that life itself becomes dull and boring. You experience no aliveness, no real enjoyment in doing what you do. It's the excitement and exhilaration that make you feel glad to be alive; the challenge, joy, stimulation, and pleasure that make life worth living.

When life is boring, you spend too many evenings sitting in front of the television set, or at a bar, or obsessively pursuing some other activity, or in one of the thousands of other places where you can hide from yourself.

This is how energy works. And you are energy. Albert Einstein discovered that matter is energy. A rock appears solid, but in reality it is pulsating molecules of energy. The same is true of wood, plants, animals, and you. Your mind is energy, your body is energy and your soul is energy. The only difference between the rock, wood, plants and your body, mind, and soul is the *vibrational rate.*

The highest vibrational rate on this earth is deep within your center at the level of the collective unconscious—the God level. The physicists have also proved that energy can't die, *it can only transform.* Scientists have isolated the smallest molecule of energy in a cloud chamber, sealed so nothing can get in and nothing can get out. The energy molecule is too small to be seen with the naked eye, but it can be photographed on ultra-high-sensitive film. When the film is projected, you see that the energy has a certain size, weight, pattern, and speed. Eventually it falls to the bottom of the cloud chamber, apparently dead. But soon the molecule transforms, returning in a new size, weight, pattern, and speed. This goes on indefinitely, just as you will go on indefinitely, lifetime after lifetime, until you have attained enlightenment by rising above fear and expressing unconditional love.

Physicists have also proved that energy can't stand still. By its very nature, energy must move forward, expanding and creating more energy. Or it must move backward, dissipating and preparing for transformation.

Since you are energy, that energy is doing the same

thing. You are either really living, experiencing aliveness and expanding, or you're slowing down, dissipating and preparing to transform (another way of saying to die and reincarnate). Aliveness generates energy, creating more energy. *What generates aliveness? CHALLENGE!*

Spiritual gurus hate this idea. They will tell you to meditate for hours a day to attain peace of mind and, eventually, enlightenment. This probably will help you attain a sense of peace, but we have scientific instruments to show what is actually happening to your mental processes. Excessive meditation will eventually cause your mind to go "flat."

In the early 1970s, a friend of mine who practiced dentistry turned to meditation in search of peace of mind. A dental practice is stressful enough, but he also had an alcoholic wife. After a few weeks of meditating for forty minutes, morning and night, the stress disappeared and he became very complacent. But his friends were soon saying, "Don, you don't seem to have anything to say to anybody anymore." He realized it was true and asked a medical doctor in his complex to run an EEG test. Upon reviewing the test the doctor said, "Don, you're stoned even when you're wide awake. You're remaining in alpha all the time."

Anyone spending approximately an hour a day or more in meditation will not return to full (wide-awake) beta consciousness. They will remain in alpha, which is "eyes-open trance." The longer you meditate, the faster it will affect your mind until you eventually become detached from reality. That doesn't mean you won't be able to function in society, but as with marijuana or Valium use, you'll separate from life right across the board—from the joy as well as from the problems. Meditation is obviously healthier for your body than marijuana or Valium, but the effects are no different: you simply become artificially peaceful.

Metaphysically speaking, it is generally agreed that until you can go through a lifetime with *total involvement* and no disharmonious attachments (fears), you will be tied to the earth, returning for continual incarnations. The key words are "total involvement." You can't be totally involved in life if you're "stoned."

Those who advocate meditation usually have an organization or a cult they want you to join or become involved in. By getting his followers to practice meditation, the leader quickly gains more control over them than he could exercise without it. The extreme result is the glassy-eyed flower-seller on the street corner, raising money for his cause or guru.

I also teach detachment, but it is *conscious detachment!* With conscious detachment you enjoy all the warmth, joy, love, and pleasure that life has to offer, but you detach from the negativity by allowing it to flow through you without affecting you—not because you are unconscious or stoned, but because you have attained self-actualized awareness.

I also teach *challenge,* and I challenge you to live dangerously. I challenge you to get involved in life, to serve others, to accomplish things, to create and to become all that you are capable of being. It is through challenge that you will experience aliveness, let go of fear and eventually attain supreme enlightenment!

In my seminars, participants often say, "I don't need to experience challenge. It isn't spiritual. I want to be part of the New Age of peace and harmony, a utopia where love will reign and competition won't exist."

I usually laugh in response and ask, "What will you do in utopia?"

Typical answers might be, "Oh, we won't have to do anything but lie around and absorb the light and listen to beautiful music." Or, "We'll just kind of resonate and vibrate with others on our soul frequency."

Then I really laugh. These ideas might relate to being in spirit, without a physical body, but I doubt even that. And I contend that if you were ever to attain such a utopia, you'd be bored to death in no time at all. You would have to generate some aliveness, some challenge! Eve would have to take a bite out of the forbidden apple, and Adam would have to create rock-and-roll music to serve as a yin-yang balance for the heavenly music.

Total security would quickly become boring. We all chase security, doing everything within our power to obtain it . . . but if we are successful, we must destroy it because there is no challenge. Even in a primary relationship between two people who love each other very much, when the relationship becomes totally secure, it becomes boring. That explains why most established, stable relationships are boring. The challenge is gone. Frequently, when the relationship is really successful, one of the partners begins an affair in an attempt to put some excitement back into their love life.

The universe functions as a yin-yang balance, resulting in a tension between opposites (yin = negative, yang = positive). We all embody dualities such as love/hate, harmony/chaos, good/evil. As a natural expression of this Law of Opposites, that which is totally successful tends to destroy itself. Historically, a country that has reached its peak begins to fragment, then collapses when unopposed. Couples rarely divorce when struggling though adversity. It's when those problems are finally resolved that they begin to destroy the relationship. An honest man attains success, then becomes corrupt. The accomplished spiritual seeker destroys what he has attained.

Intuitively, we all know this, and yet we must express our yin-yang duality because human beings are energy structures, and this tension is necessary for the structure to exist.

Look at life! You probably won't have to look far to see that what I'm saying is true. We know it subconsciously, not consciously; this may explain why most people never allow themselves to become totally successful. If they do, they'll have to destroy their success because there will no longer be any challenge. From a higher perspective this isn't good or bad, it's just what is. An automobile battery offers a good analogy. It consists of a series of metal plates—one is charged positively, the next negatively, the next positively, and so on. Energy is created by the interaction between the positive and negative plates. The negative plate isn't bad any more than the positive plate is good.

In converting this awareness into action, the idea is to replace the negative (yin) tension with a positive challenge. We have to consciously direct challenge in a way that minimizes real danger while achieving the required yin-yang balance. This is usually accomplished by *wise risking.* In other words, *no matter how successful you are, always give yourself new and greater challenges in all areas of your life:* your relationship, hobbies, career, spirituality, and even your service to others and to the planet. *Always create new challenges for yourself.*

If you don't create new challenges, your energy is stagnating—dissipating and readying itself to transform. Remember, energy can't stand still; it must, by its very nature, move either forward or backward.

Maybe it is time for you to begin living a little more dangerously and start breaking the many chains of illusion. I would suggest you experience the following process in an altered state of consciousness.

Aliveness Process

(Do the induction first.) I am relaxed and at ease and ready to objectively explore my life and my present levels of aliveness. Aliveness is excitement and enjoyment of my experiences. It's the blood-pumping exhilaration that makes me feel glad to be alive.

And I will now answer each question "yes" or "no." First I'll explore my career.

Do I presently experience aliveness in my career? Yes or no.

Is there any real challenge in my career? Yes or no.

Am I growing in my career? Yes or no.

Am I satisfied in my career? Yes or no.

All right, if I answered "no" to many of these questions, I am either not living up to my career potential or else my career energy is stagnating. I remind myself that energy cannot stand still and stagnation leads to self-destruction. So, if there is no real challenge in my career, what could I do to create challenge and aliveness? *(Long pause.)*

And now it is time to explore my primary relationship. *(If you don't have a primary relationship, but desire one, use your time to focus upon why you haven't created the space in your life to manifest a relationship.)*

Do I presently experience aliveness in my primary relationship? Yes or no.

Is there still challenge in my primary relationship? Yes or no.

Are there stimulating activities, other than sex, that we share together? Yes or no.

Am I growing in my relationship? Yes or no.

Am I satisfied with my relationship? Yes or no.

Again, if I answered "no" to many of these questions I am stagnating or not living up to my potential for a warm, fulfilling, joyful relationship in which there is mutual personal growth. So, if there is no real challenge in my relationship, what could I do to create challenge and aliveness? *(Long pause.)*

Now I will explore my sex life . . .

Do I presently experience aliveness in my sex life? Yes or no.

Is there any real challenge in my sex life? Yes or no.

Am I repressing my sexual desires in any way? Yes or no.

Do I communicate my sexual desire to my partner? Yes or no.

Am I satisfied with my sex life? Yes or no.

If I answered "no" to many of these questions I am repressing, or dissipating, my sexual energy. So the question is, what could I do to create aliveness in my sex life? And before I answer that question, I need to be aware that sexual conduct should never cause pain or harm to others, or turbulence or disturbance in ourselves. With that awareness in mind, what could I do to create aliveness in my sex life? *(Long pause.)*

The next questions are about spiritual searching.

Do I experience aliveness in my spiritual involvements and seeking? Yes or no.

Is there still a challenge in my spiritual search? Yes or no.

Am I still open to exploring new spiritual potentials, concepts, and ideas? Yes or no.

Am I really growing spiritually? Yes or no.

And if I answered "no" to many of these questions, I am probably stagnating spiritually; the question to ask myself then is, what can I do to generate challenge and aliveness in my spiritual life? *(Long pause.)*

The last question has to do with service . . .

Am I presently serving others or the planet in any

way that results in a sense of aliveness and satisfaction? Yes or no.

If I answered "no" to this question, what could I do to become involved and experience aliveness by serving the planet? *(Long pause.)*

This process is a good indicator as to how much challenge I am experiencing in my life. Am I experiencing aliveness, or is it time to consider living dangerously? Maybe it is time to reject the commands of power . . . to reject the dictates of society and public opinion and create some new challenges in my life. *(Long pause for meditation time.) (Awaken.)*

When you begin to question yourself and go deeper within for the answers, things start to happen in your life. Simple answers lead to overall awareness and small changes lead to major changes. I challenge you to challenge yourself.

CHAPTER

15

Putting It All Together (With Case History Dialogues)

The following dialogues were taken from tape recordings of my Master of Life Seminar Trainings conducted in various cities throughout the country. Notes taken at the seminars were also used to accurately re-create interactions between me and the participants. The names have been changed, and in some situations, dialogues have been combined or edited to avoid repetition.

The seminars consist of short, powerful talks, altered-state-of-consciousness explorations and processing sessions. Participants are always invited to question or share their experiences. They may raise their hands to interact with me if they desire, but there is no pressure to share individually. I do encourage all to leap into the unknown to find their true selves. The true self is discovered when the false (fear-based) self is renounced. To help them accomplish that goal, I must jolt those attending the seminar out of their intellectual ruts, passé notions, and the viewpoints and convictions that are restricting them.

Outside the seminar room setting, some of the communications may appear cold and unfeeling. In reality, they are a form of the Zen teacher/student interaction, and I have only one goal in mind: to create the space for the participant to help himself by finding his own answers within. And I must do this even at the cost of incurring his dislike and the dislike of the other attendees.

1.

MARK

"I just can't accept the concept of unconditional love," Mark said. He was a New Yorker in his mid-thirties, and his glasses gave him an intellectual look. "How can you expect me to love everyone else on this planet with unconditional love, when I've never even seen two people capable of loving each other unconditionally?"

"Don't equate unconditional love with romantic love, Mark," I replied. "The esoteric response would be to equate unconditional love to the way a spiritual Master would love. Think of him as a flower in a garden. You pass by and inhale the fragrance of the flower. The flower didn't send the fragrance to you specifically; it was there even when no one was there to enjoy it. And if no one were ever to pass by, the fragrance would still be there."

"Give me a break," Mark responded. His expression was pained.

"Okay, let's look at it from another perspective. Can you perceive unconditional love as the acceptance of other people without judgment . . . without expectations . . . without blame?"

"I guess," he replied, "but I don't think that's very realistic."

"I think logic is very realistic, Mark," I said, stepping off the stage and walking up the aisle until I was standing only a few feet from him.

"Logic?" He shook his head, denial implicit in every movement.

"Mark, you can't change anyone else, no matter how badly you might want to. Oh, sure, you might tell your lover, 'you're going to change or I'm going to leave.' The threat might work . . . for a while. But she will then be repressing who she really is, and eventually the repression will erupt, very likely in an even less desirable way. You can fight her and become upset and make your life miserable, but she won't really change. Or, you can just calmly accept her the way she is. *The outcome is the same either way.* It isn't logical to get upset when there is no value in doing so. If you can't change her, you might as well accept her as she is . . . if you want to continue the relationship. Simple logic, right?"

"Yeah, but there are a lot of people I can't accept as they are," Mark replied, his expression showing disapproval.

"Mark, can't you get that it doesn't matter what you think? You can upset yourself about what is, or not upset yourself. The other people will still be just what they are. Your refusal to accept them only generates subconscious negativity that you'll have to balance in the future, without changing a thing. In other words, you have a choice. You can make things worse for yourself or not make things worse for yourself, but either way you can't change anything else. It's not very logical to choose negativity."

Mark just stared at me.

"Wouldn't it be better to just accept others unconditionally than to program your subconscious mind with negativity that will have to be balanced? Many years ago I wrote what I call the Eleven Basic Human Rights. Right number three deals with this issue: *It is your right to be what you are without changing your ideas or behavior to satisfy someone else.* Do you want to have to change your ideas or behavior to be the way other people want you to be, Mark?"

"No!"

"Then how can you expect anyone else to change for you? Any halfway self-actualized person is going to grant that right to others and demand it for himself. I've asked thousands of people in seminars if there is anyone in the audience who doesn't want that right for themselves. No one has ever put up his hand. But, let's carry this a little further. If you want this human right for yourself, and you are willing to give it to everyone else, then everyone else is *already perfect,* aren't they? And you're perfect, too."

"Perfect?" Mark replied. "I've got an ex-wife who's hardly perfect." A loud murmur filled the seminar room as the other participants nodded their heads in agreement.

"Think about it, Mark. If you're not asking them to change, you give them the freedom to be who they are. They may not live up to your idea of what is best for them. You may see them as complete jerks. But you have to respect them for what they are, not for what you want them to be. From the perspective of human rights, everyone is perfect just as they are. You need to give up all your anger, resentments, hostility, and blame. None of the fear-based emotions are even logical under the circumstances we've just discussed."

"I get very stuck on the word 'perfect,'" Mark replied.

"Then how about saying your ex-wife is *acceptable*

as she is?" I asked. "If you can't easily say she is acceptable as she is, you are making her wrong in comparison to your viewpoint. That's not logical. It's not in your best interest and it certainly isn't unconditional love. You don't see the other people in your life as they really are. No one in this room has ever seen anyone as they really are. You see them through a veil of opinions and conclusions—your viewpoint. So, you certainly don't see them accurately.

"Remember a time when a friend fell in love, and you could not understand what he saw in her," I continued. "Well, your viewpoints were different. Everybody sees everybody differently, and none of the perceptions are accurate. We are dealing with illusions. *Illusions.* Other people's reactions to you are nothing but statements of their viewpoints, which have nothing to do with facts, with the way things actually are. So, if human interactions are based on illusory perceptions, why bother to judge others at all. It isn't even logical."

Mark shook his head slowly and sat down.

2.

JEAN

"Surely, that's not all there is to unconditional love?" asked Jean, an attractive woman in her late twenties. She was dressed in a conservative suit, looking very much the young executive.

"I think we could discuss unconditional love all day and not begin to cover the subject," I replied. "Ancient Zen teaching offers what is called the Three Principal Aspects of the Path to Supreme Enlightenment. First is *the determination to be freed from the cyclical existence of reincarnation.* This means you make a conscious decision to live your life in a way that generates only virtuous or neutral karma. Second is *the correct view of emptiness.* I teach this as conscious detachment. The primary way to end suffering and attain peace of mind is to detach from negativity, allowing it to flow through you without affecting you. Third is *to develop an altruistic mind of enlightenment,* which I teach as the expression of unconditional love. If you examine these three steps to becoming a Master, I believe you will see that they can be simplified to the concept of letting go of fear and expressing unconditional love."

"Without fear, wouldn't all our thoughts, words and deeds be loving?" Jean asked, her voice expressing conviction.

I nodded in agreement. "Unconditional love transcends everything else. It transcends religion. It transcends philosophy. It is the only tangible thing in life, and everything else is illusion. We don't need the Ten Commandments, or Buddha's Eight-Fold Plan. We don't need preachers or philosophers or gurus. All we need is the awareness of this goal: to evolve to the point where we can express unconditional love in response to every situation we encounter.

"Simple, isn't it? But if you can accept this idea, you are far ahead of most people on this planet. People as a whole need ritual and dogma. We are conditioned to believe that the answers are hidden and only known to the wise who have spent their lives studying to attain awareness. Or those who are somehow special enough to succeed in channeling wisdom from the spiritual realms.

"Well, guess what? That isn't what is. And yet, the guru types who have spent their lives searching for the answers want you to think this. This assures them of their position and power . . . and probably their daily bread."

* * *

3.

WALTER

"You seem to be pretty judgmental toward gurus. That isn't expressing unconditional love," said Walter, a man in his fifties wearing a brightly colored running suit.

"Not judging others does not mean that you ignore faults or mistakes, Walter. You don't turn off your brain and stop deciding what works and what doesn't. Gurus sell their followers a future of hope while cheating them of present enjoyment. They also use conversion techniques to assure loyalty. If you need to experience a guru as a karmic lesson, that's what is. But when you wise up, remember, wisdom erases karma."

4.

MARIA

"I can't see where there is any difference between unconditional love and human love as we all experience it with those closest to us. Wouldn't we ideally just expand this love to encompass all mankind?" asked Maria. She was in her late thirties or early forties, wearing a hand-woven shawl and American Indian jewelry.

"Human love is usually a form of attachment, Maria," I replied. "Attachment to your mate, your parents, your children, or your best friend. Sure you have a feeling of love and compassion, but because this love is related to attachment, it cannot include the other people in the world. Plus, most human love is motivated by selfishness. Because this is my mate, my parent, my child, my friend, I love them. That is attachment, which is possessiveness, which is really fear. Most of us are jealous, possessive, envious, and yet we talk about love. If you are possessive and envious, can you really love, or are you just protecting what gives you pleasure? That's fear! Most of the romantic human love I've observed is based on a fear of losing the loved one. And where there is fear, there is aggression. So, most relationships involve a great deal of aggression."

"You may be right about some of my relationships, but not all of them," Maria responded. "I think it's possible to look upon human love a little more positively than that."

I smiled and nodded in response. "I've always liked a quote of Stewart Emery's: 'Love is when I am concerned with your relationship with your own life, rather than your relationship with mine. I love you, knowing that if your relationship with yourself works, your relationship with me will automatically work, and if your relationship with yourself and your own life doesn't work, your relationship with me doesn't work either.'

"It's beautiful. It's unconditional love in action. We have to stop judging those we love and care about, and we have to stop judging everyone else, too. Here is something else to tell someone you love, 'You're perfect just the way you are. Does the way you are work for you?' Could you say that to your mate or lover? To your parents? To your close friends? If you can't, then you are judging the other person and you want them to change."

Maria looked me right in the eyes. "I see that I've got to grasp all this intellectually first, and then hopefully it will filter down into emotional acceptance. It's all fear, isn't it?"

"It's almost all fear, but clarity of intent has a lot to do with it. Going back to the Three Principal Aspects of the Path to Supreme Enlightenment, the first is the determination to be freed from the cyclical existence of reincarnation. *Determination* is dependent on *clarity of intent—knowing what you really want!* Not only is your spiritual evolution dependent on clarity of intent, the primary reason people are not happy is because they lack that clarity. That's why they don't have what they want and why their lives don't work. How can you attain a goal if you don't know exactly what you want? To unleash the unlimited power of your mind, you need to know what you want. This involves three steps: 1. Determine what you want. 2. Discover what is blocking you from getting it. (Use altered-state exploratory techniques if necessary.) 3. Decide what you are willing to pay in order to get what you want. The cost of enlightenment will be measured in effort and sacrifice."

5.

BLAKE

Blake raised his hand hesitantly. When I recognized him, he stood up slowly and continued to look at the ground as he spoke into the microphone. "All this talk about love just reminds me of how badly I've messed up my life. After three divorces, I'm not about to get involved with another woman and take a chance on human or unconditional love."

"Well, Blake, you can choose not to play, or you can choose to transform the way you view your past," I said.

"How can I view three divorces as anything but failures?" he said, still not looking at me.

"There is no such thing as failure, Blake. Remember when you were learning to ride a bicycle? You fell off a lot. Maybe you fell off nine times before you succeeded on the tenth attempt. Okay, so you needed nine failures to achieve success. In reality, each failure was a small success leading to the ultimate success. So, maybe you should think of each divorce as a small success—necessary growth experiences leading toward a self-actualized relationship.

"Sadly, we all learn through pain. We learn not to touch a hot stove by burning our fingers a few times. The same with the way we handle relationships or anything else. Maybe you needed the pain of three divorces to learn what generates harmony and disharmony in a marriage."

"Transforming my viewpoint on my marriages isn't quite that easy," Blake responded softly into the microphone. "Maybe I don't really understand transformation."

"Transformation is rising above or going beyond the limits ordinarily imposed by form. Transformation is another way of saying 'self-actualization.' It means to house a different essence in the same form. If I could change a peach into a pear, that wouldn't be transformation. If I could take a peach and turn it into a peach that tasted like a pear, that would be transformation. To a person who has experienced transformation, the world remains exactly as it was before. What has changed is his viewpoint on those circumstances, the way he relates to his world—the immediate circumstance hasn't changed at all. When you transform your viewpoint, you rise above your fear of the problem. The situation is the same, but you've stopped resisting it."

6.

JOANNE

"I'd like to transform the way I experience my husband, but the fact is, he's a bastard. He drinks too much and never does what he says he'll do. It's been going on since we got married seven years ago," Joanne said. She was a small woman in her late twenties, dressed in a sweater and jeans, her movements expressing assertiveness.

"In all the time you've been together, has he ever changed, Joanne?" I asked.

"No, not a bit," she said, her voice brimming with distaste.

"Do you want to remain with him?"

"Of course, I do. I really love him," she said.

"Do you spend a lot of time dwelling on your situation?" I asked. "Do you relate your soap opera adventures with your husband to your girlfriends? Do you continually argue with your husband about the way he is?"

She nodded sheepishly.

"Do you have anything else very exciting going on in your life right now, Joanne?"

"No," she said.

"It sounds to me like your husband provides the aliveness in your life. There is a payoff for you in keeping things exactly the way they are. If your relationship worked smoothly, you wouldn't have anything to complain or fight about and your life would become mundane. Your mind couldn't handle that. The human mind seeks challenge and excitement. If you don't provide it, your mind will. So you might consider creating some positive challenges in your life that generate aliveness and allow you to get off your relationship issues.

"But let's get back to the concept of transforming the way you experience your husband. You've been attempting to change him for seven years and it hasn't worked yet, and Joanne, I can guarantee you it never will work. Now, if your husband ever decides to change himself, that's a different story. Of course, he can change then, but the bottom line is, you can't change him. Look at your choices—you can either leave him or you can stay with him and accept him as he is."

"Some choice!" Joanne responded.

"You can make yourself miserable by resisting your husband, or you can stop resisting him and use the time and emotion you've been wasting in some positive way. Can't you see the wisdom in that?"

"Yes, but I don't like it," she said.

"Like it or not, that's what is, Joanne. You want to remain in the situation. You can remain and fight it, or you can transform the way you've been experiencing it. You can say, 'Well, that's the way John is,' and accept it. One path is resistance, and it results in negative subconscious programming that is sure to generate undesirable results. The other path is conscious detachment, allowing the negativity to flow through you without affecting you. And when you stop resisting your husband, you may find that he will respond to you differently. Transform the way you view your relationship, add some new challenges to your life, and you may find that the old problems will be resolved on their own."

7.

ALICE

"How does all this relate to my situation?" Alice asked. "My entire life is presently dedicated to helping my twenty-two-year-old daughter. She has totally messed up her life and she's miserable. I'm trying to help her but she seems to resent everything I do. She thinks I'm interfering."

"It appears to me that what is causing your problem, Alice, is you don't want your daughter to believe that."

"Of course not," she replied. "All I'm trying to do is help." The woman standing before me was in her mid-forties, conservatively dressed and wearing expensive jewelry.

"I realize you mean well, Alice. But you need to get that you are acting in your own self-interest by responding to your daughter in a way you feel a mother *should* respond. You are *shoulding* on yourself and your daughter and making everyone miserable because of it. Get rid of your expectations about what should be and things may improve."

At this point in our dialogue, Alice started crying and said, "I just don't want my daughter to be so miserable."

"Alice, accept what is," I said. "No matter how much you love someone, there are times when you can do nothing to save another person from pain. Your daughter's pain is her choice and she is the only one who can choose not to experience it."

"Well, isn't there anything I can do?" she asked, her voice soft and pleading.

"I don't know what you can do. I do know that helping others often takes away their power. You give them a crutch and they never learn to stand on their own two feet. We grow through our pain; none of us would have the strength we have today if we hadn't experienced the pain in our past. Granted, it is certainly wiser to learn through love and wisdom, yet few of us have really discovered that yet. It's what unconditional love is all about. I advocate helping your loved ones to help themselves, so they retain their power and increase their self-esteem. If you really love them that will be more important than the ego satisfaction you get by living up to your self-image of a good mother.

"Be compassionate. You do this automatically when you love someone, yet there are other factors to be considered—in particular, three questions: 1. Does your daughter accept responsibility for her life? 2. Is she willing to solve her problems? 3. Does she know what to do? If the answer to the first two questions is no, there is little you can do that will serve her. If the answer to the first two questions is yes, she probably doesn't really need your help, but this is where your assistance could be of value. How can you assist your daughter by giving her the space to help herself? Be creative in your search for solutions."

8.

CANDACE

Candace was a beautiful woman in her early thirties, dressed in white slacks and a bulky white sweater. She requested the microphone to talk about an affair she had had recently. "My husband forgave me," she said, attempting to discipline her voice to maintain control. "Actually, he really showed unconditional love, and since then everything has been much better between us. But my problem is, I can't forgive myself. I guess it's my Christian upbringing, but I feel like I broke one of the Ten Commandments and it just haunts me."

I told her to look at it as a learning experience, but she remained stuck on the Ten Commandments as the only way to view morality. So I explained, "If you were to explore the Six Paramitas of the Bodhisattva in Buddhist teachings, you would find that adultery is one of the ten precepts. And it is explained as meaning that the person having sex with another must consider his own happiness, that of his companion, and that of the third person who will be most affected by his act.

If these three concerned people can be satisfied, then sex falls within the natural law of human beings.

"Sexual misconduct also comes under the second pillar of dharma—the field of purifying action. In this case, it can most easily be understood as refraining from the kinds of sensuality that cause pain and harm to others, or turbulence or disturbance in ourselves."

"I guess knowing that helps," Candace replied, "but I need to forgive myself. I think I'm subconsciously doing things to punish myself."

"Subconscious self-punishment is very real," I agreed. "The past guilt causes you to draw negative situations into your field of experience. To forgive the past, you must release it and begin to accept positive new programming." I turned to the entire seminar audience. "I'd like everyone to explore this, because self-forgiveness relates to everyone. Close your eyes and take a few moments to think about the primary areas of your life that aren't working—the areas you would most like to change." *(Long pause.)*

"It is very likely that you have subconsciously created these situations to balance something you've done in the past. If you don't know the cause, you can find it in a 'Back to the Cause Regression' *(see Chapter 4)*. Once you know the cause, as in Candace's case, you can use self-hypnosis to reprogram your subconscious mind.

"Technique 1: After you have induced an altered state of consciousness, create a mental movie in which someone descends from the clouds to talk to you. It could be God, Buddha, Christ, your guardian angel, a Master or guide. Then imagine them telling you, *'You have punished yourself long enough. You are forgiven for everything that transpired in the past, even that which you cannot consciously remember. You are forgiven, and it is time that you forgive yourself.'* Make the mental movie real. It is very powerful subconscious programming. Also create visualizations in which you *feel* forgiven and are no longer manifesting disharmonious effects.

"Technique 2: Use this alone or combined with Technique 1. In an altered state, chant a mantra over and over, hundreds of times. Here are a couple of examples. *'I forgive myself. From the bottom of my heart, I now forgive myself for all the past mistakes I have made, even those I do not remember.' 'From this moment on, I no longer punish myself. I now create the positive life I want to live, exactly the way I want it to be.'"*

9.

BETH

"I've been listening, but I still don't see how I can respond with unconditional love to a husband who is always picking fights with me." Beth was fortyish, with short hair and casual, trendy clothes.

"How do you respond to him?" I asked.

"Well, I stand up for myself. I fight back. Everybody has a right to defend themselves," she said.

"I agree," I said. "Self-defense is a basic human right. How long have you and your husband been fighting back and forth like this?"

"Since shortly after we got married, about nine years ago."

"Has your relationship improved as a result of all this fighting?" I asked.

"No," she replied. "If anything, it has probably deteriorated."

"Obviously, Beth, what you're doing isn't working, is it? You'd like to change him and he doesn't change. So, are you willing to approach the problem in a different way?"

"That depends," she replied warily.

"On what?" I asked.

"Well, I'm certainly not going to let him get away with attacking me."

"You mean, you're not going to let him be right?"

"No, not when he's wrong!" Her voice was very assertive.

"Beth, for years you've been attempting to be right and you're obviously losing the game. Beth gets to be right. Beth's relationship deteriorates. Beth gets a divorce. I don't have your answers, Beth, but if I were in your shoes and I wanted to remain married, I'd at least explore my potential to transform the way I experience the relationship."

"How else can you experience it, except by what's right and wrong?" she questioned.

"Beth, there is no such thing as right and wrong in a situation like this. There is only what you call 'right' and 'wrong.' Even if several of us agree to call your husband 'wrong,' that doesn't *make* him wrong—it only makes him what *we* call wrong. It doesn't change what he actually is. What is right to you could be totally wrong to Walter, sitting in the chair next to you."

"Okay," Beth said, obviously thinking deeply about what I was saying. "I don't want to get divorced. I really do love my husband, but he attacks me and I hate it. Most people would react the same way I do."

"Maybe you could transform the way you view his attacks," I said. "What if you viewed the attacker as being afraid. No one attacks unless they feel threatened somehow. Attack is a defense, and it is rooted in fear. If you can change your point of view and see him as fearful, realize too that fear is really a call for help, which you can probably interpret as a request for love."

Beth stared at me for a few moments and then

asked, "But how could my knowing that change anything?"

"I don't know," I admitted, "but maybe once you grasp this awareness it wouldn't be so important to be right. Maybe instead of attacking in return, you could respond with love. What is the worst that would happen if you responded with love?"

"Well, it couldn't be any worse than it is now," she sighed. "It would probably be better. There probably wouldn't be any fights. But then he might just go on like he always does. But . . . I guess I don't have anything to lose by trying, do I?"

10.

LINDA

"I really was upset by the way you responded to Martha a few minutes ago. She was telling a story that made me cry and I think you responded very coldly. You made her cry," Linda said, one hand expressing anxiety by twisting her necklace. She was probably in her late thirties, overweight, and wearing a one-piece flowered dress.

"You obviously have expectations about how I should respond to other people and I didn't live up to your expectations, Linda. You wanted me to be the way you wanted me to be, and when I wasn't, you got upset. Can you get how your resistance to *what is* causes you unnecessary anxiety?"

"I don't have any anxiety," she snapped back.

"Then why are you scowling at me and clenching your fist?" I asked. "Your body language says you're upset. Linda, this training room is a mirror for your life. How does this situation relate to your behavior in your day-to-day life? Perhaps you want everybody to live up to your expectations. What about your husband? You want your husband to be what you want him to be, don't you?"

"So what? Most people want that," she said defiantly.

"Right," I agreed. "And that is one of the reasons why their lives don't work very well—there is no unconditional love. When you realize you can't change others and you begin to accept them as they are, you stop resisting what is. Then your life will work better. But let's get back to the fact that you're upset with me because I made Martha cry. Did you want me to respond to Martha with pity?"

"YES!" she said, speaking very loudly into the microphone.

"Do you think that your desire to have me react that way will cause me to change? Do you think you can change me?"

"No," she said, her eyes narrow and her jaw set.

"Then why resist what is, Linda? Why resist what you can't do anything about? It is your resistance to life that causes your suffering. If you had accepted that Richard does what he does without getting upset, you could have saved yourself this turmoil, couldn't you?"

"I just wanted you to know how I felt," she snapped.

"But I don't care how you felt, Linda. I wouldn't take anything you said to me personally, good or bad. Nobody cares how you feel when you're bitching, Linda. Does that bother you?"

"Some people certainly care. My husband cares."

"No, maybe they pretend to care, to keep from setting you off any more than you already are. But they don't care."

Linda stopped talking, intensified her scowl, and planted both hands firmly on her hips.

"Okay, Linda, let's go back to my reaction to

Martha. I'm certainly not going to pity Martha or anyone else in this seminar ballroom. If I did, I would be supporting their negative programming. Also, let me tell you a story that is often used in human-potential trainings. It's about sympathy, empathy, and compassion. Let's assume you are walking along a road by the ocean and you come upon a drowning man. First, you can exhibit sympathy by jumping into the ocean and drowning with him. We call that a 'pity party.' Second, you can show a lot of empathy and sit down and begin to moan and cry and carry on about the poor drowning man. Third, you can show compassion and do something about it. You might find a rope to throw him, or run and find someone who knows how to swim. Ideally, when you find yourself experiencing compassion for another human being, you will assist by creating conditions within which they can choose to alleviate their own problem."

11.

DIANA

Diana was thirty-four, very warm and attractive. Never married, she was a college graduate and a computer specialist. "I really want to establish a good relationship with a man," she said. "I've been career oriented but now I'm ready to share my life. I'd like to get married. I date several times a week, but the problem is, I just can't seem to find the right man. I'm in a position to meet many eligible men, and several I've dated have wanted to get serious, but they all have flaws I couldn't live with."

"Let's say you could find the perfect man, Diana. What would he be like?" I asked.

"He would be good-looking, at least six feet tall, preferably blond. I can't stand men who are overweight. He would have a lucrative, well-established career and be a responsible person. I also want someone who is morally adult. Since we're talking about ideal, I guess I should add that I'd like him to be kind of a 'white knight.'"

"What does responsible mean?" I asked.

"Someone who fulfills his obligations," she explained. "Someone who does what he says he will do and has a good credit rating, which at least provides some proof of responsibility."

"What does morally adult mean?" I asked.

"Someone who doesn't have any kinky ideas, and is satisfied with one woman. Someone I could count on not to have affairs," she said firmly.

"What are kinky ideas, Diana?" I asked.

"You know, weird sex. Half the men I've met are open to threesomes or more . . . women with women. Some of them think it is more creative to make love on the kitchen table than the normal way."

"The normal way?" I asked.

"Yes," she snapped. "Normal sex in bed. Regular positions. I don't want to keep on with this."

"Why not, Diana?"

"It seems to me you're getting too personal. Looking for perverse information."

"Does the subject of sex make you uncomfortable, Diana?"

"I don't think sex needs to be discussed. The whole world is obsessed with it. A normal man would only want to make love once or twice a week."

"Would you look forward to those times, Diana, or would you sexually comply for the sake of the man?"

"It would be all right," she said. "I know men need sex."

"Don't women need sex?" I asked.

"Some seem to more than others," she said in an irritated tone of voice. "But if they were fulfilled in other ways, I doubt that they would. If they had a successful career, for instance."

"Okay, Diana, another question about your ideal man. What do you mean by a 'white knight'?"

She smiled and said, "A man who would sweep me off my feet with flowers and romance. He'd make the important decisions and carry me off into his world."

"Do you know anyone who lives up to your image of an ideal man?" I asked. "Anyone, anywhere, married or not?"

Diana remained silent, obviously thinking, for several seconds. "No, I guess I don't," she finally said.

"Well, Diana, what if you could find a man who fulfilled your ideal image in every way, except he had a fetish for occasionally having sex on the kitchen table?"

She frowned at me in disgust and shook her head "no." So I continued to question her. "What if he was ideal in every way except that he was about twenty pounds overweight?"

"I can't stand men who are overweight," she curtly replied.

"Let's look at this another way," I said. "Let's assume you found the ideal man and the two of you fall in love and get married. What would change in your life that's undesirable to you? For everything you want, there is a price to pay in either time, money, effort, or sacrifice. What would you have to give up?"

Diana stared at the floor, thinking, for several seconds. "My freedom to come and go as I please. And, I'd have to respond sexually. I know I'd have to compromise in areas such as food, entertainment, friends, social events, vacations . . . EVERYTHING!"

"Freedom, sex, responsibilities, compromise! How do you really feel about making those adjustments, Diana? Be straight!"

She smiled sheepishly and said, "Not real good, to be perfectly honest. It almost sounds like it's more trouble than it's worth, doesn't it?" She laughed.

"Okay, Diana, are you getting that you don't want a relationship? You have no clarity of intent, and there are too many *negative payoffs*. A negative payoff is when you say you want something to be different than it is, but consciously or subconsciously you block the desired goal because there is some kind of payoff in maintaining the status quo. You also have unrealistic expectations and are obviously filled with fear in regard to establishing a relationship."

Tears began to well up in Diana's eyes. "But I do," she stammered. "I really do want a relationship. I would love to be married like all my girlfriends. Something inside me is almost obsessed with the idea. A girl my age *should* be married!"

"Should be married?" I asked. "Who says so? Where is that written?"

"All my girlfriends are married," she sobbed.

"Diana, we've already discussed many of the obvious blocks to a relationship and unconditional love. Maybe we've touched on the reason you feel the way you do about a relationship, but I'd like to make sure. I realize this is a big issue for you, and obviously you're experiencing a great deal of inner conflict. I want you to understand the cause of the conflict. Are you willing to do some regression work?"

She readily agreed and I hypnotized Diana and directed her to go back to the cause of her conflict with men—back to the cause of fearing a loss of freedom, fearing sex, responsibilities, and compromise. Once her eyes began to move rapidly behind her partially closed eyelids, I asked her where she was and what she was doing. She responded very slowly, and her voice was different. It sounded tired, emotionless. "I'm in a small cabin . . . cooking, I think. Yes."

"You have the power and ability to look around," I told her. "Describe the cabin to me, and tell me if there is anyone else there with you."

Several seconds passed before she answered. "My man is at the table. The room is very small—there are a couple of windows, but they are shut and barred to keep the cold out. It is winter and it is very cold, even inside. I'm wrapped in something, but I'm still shivering."

"Can you tell me the year? The current year?"

"Dunno," she said softly, and seemed to be confused. "1842 or maybe '43 or '44. I lose track. It doesn't matter."

"Tell me about your life," I requested.

"Not much to tell," she said, clearing her throat as if she were about to spit. "Harold hunts and I grow a few things. We survive. That's all you can hope for."

"How old are you?"

"Ahhh . . . I guess forty-one or forty-two."

"How long have you lived here in this cabin?"

"Oh, fifteen years . . . no that's not right, closer to eighteen, I guess. But when I was young I lived in New York City and it was wonderful. Life was gay and happy. My mistake in life was going west."

"Did you meet Harold in the West?" I asked.

"Yes," she said. "After my family died. He took me in and fed me in exchange for favors."

"What do you mean, 'favors'?" I asked.

"You know . . . favors. He has his way with me," she said, almost mumbling.

"Tell me about Harold. Describe him to me," I said.

"Not much to tell. He's a big man and he hunts. I cook and we survive."

"Is Harold big and also fat?" I asked.

"Oh yes, very, very fat," she said.

After Diana was awakened from the regression I said, "Obviously, your subconscious mind has been programmed by this past lifetime. Your conscious and subconscious are out of alignment. Subconsciously, you fear that if you establish a relationship with a man, you'll once again have to experience the drudgery and depression that were part of your previous incarnation. The past-life fear is blocking your desire to experience unconditional love in the present."

"Will knowing the cause help me to let go of my fears about relationships?" Diana asked anxiously.

"Sometimes knowing the cause will immediately alleviate the effect—that's what therapists hope for. But if it doesn't, I agree with the new Zen therapies that a change in behavior will lead to a change in attitude. In light of your new awareness, Diana, you must ask yourself a lot of questions about the reason you want a relationship. Do you want it because you think you should have a relationship, or because your girlfriends are all married? That's a *faulty assumption.* But if you decide you want a relationship because you are really ready to share your life and to establish a bonding that will allow for mutual growth, then you must *confront your fears and act anyway.* Your fears are from a previous lifetime and do not necessarily relate to today."

All of this takes us back to my original assertion as to why we are here on the earth at this time. It's all a process to learn to let go of fear, and to express unconditional love. And in the process, everyone has the right to seek happiness, end suffering, and attain peace of mind. The Dalai Lama offered some wonderful wisdom on this subject during his visit to the United States a few years ago:

"In a sense, the spiritual practitioner is actually a soldier engaged in combat. With what enemies does he or she fight? Internal ones. Ignorance, anger, attachment, and pride are the ultimate enemies; they are not outside, but within, and must be fought with the weapons of wisdom and concentration. Wisdom is the bullet. The ammunition is concentration. The calm abiding of the mind is the weapon for firing it."

Unconditional Love Hypnosis Script

(Do the induction first.) And I am now relaxed and centered. I feel at peace, in balance and in harmony. A quietness of spirit permeates my body and mind as I now begin to explore the concept of unconditional love. I am here on earth to let go of fear and to learn to express unconditional love. Unconditional love transcends everything else. It transcends religion . . . it transcends philosophy. It is the only tangible thing in life; everything else is illusion.

And I have the power and ability to release the unconditional love that lies within me . . . and to express unconditional love in response to everyone and every situation. Unconditional love awakens my heart and my soul; from this moment on, my very essence is transformed. I now reflect the spirit of peace, light, balance, and harmony. I am love and I express love in everything I think, say, and do. And these words are communicated to every level of my body and mind . . . and so it is.

I now create a mental movie in which I perceive myself responding to a difficult situation with unconditional love. I will make this fantasy real and perceive every detail in my mind. *(Two minutes or more of silence.)*

And I have just seen my own reality. From this moment on, I express unconditional love in everything I think, say, and do. And I am now going to use a mantra technique to communicate and saturate my subconscious mind with the awareness of my transformation. I will repeat the words in unison, silently in my mind: "I am the spirit of peace, light, balance, and harmony." *(Repeat ten times or more.)*

And here is another mantra: "I now express unconditional love in everything I think, say, and do." *(Repeat ten times or more.)*

All right, let's project another mantra: "Unconditional love awakens my heart and awakens my soul." *(Repeat ten times or more.)*

That's right! Unconditional love does awaken my heart and my soul. And I am now going to give myself some key trigger words that I can use to elicit a conditioned response. Any time in my daily life that I find myself encountering a difficult person or negative situation, I will simply stop what I am doing, close my eyes, take a deep breath, and say these words quietly to myself . . . "unconditional love." The words "unconditional love" are a key to my subconscious mind. When I say these words, I will actually feel the essence of unconditional love awakening my heart and soul. And I will then express this love in everything I think, say, and do. The words "unconditional love" have become a suggestion that will be totally effective in evoking a conditioned response. And every time I hear this suggestion, and every time I use my "unconditional love" programming, it will become more and more effective.

I create a mental movie in which I perceive myself using my "unconditional love" programming, responding to the most difficult situations very lovingly, with peace, balance, and harmony. *(Two minutes or more of silence.) (Awaken.)*

SECTION

III

Altered States of Consciousness

CHAPTER

16

"The Technique"

Altered State of Consciousness General Induction and Awakening

(First, use deep breathing to relax your body and mind. Take a very deep in-breath, and hold it for as long as you comfortably can. Then let the breath out slowly through slightly parted lips; this allows you to retain the moisture in your mouth. When you think there is no air left in your lungs, contract your stomach muscles and force out any that remains. Then repeat the process. Do this diaphragm breathing for two to five minutes before you begin the body relaxation. When you begin to relax your physical body, play the role, play the part and imagine your body relaxing in response to the suggestions.)

BODY RELAXATION

The relaxing power is now entering the toes of both of my feet at the same time. It is moving right on down into the ball . . . into my arches . . . into my heels, and up into my ankles. Completely relaxed. Completely relaxed. And the relaxing power now moves on up my legs to my knees, relaxing all the muscles as it goes . . . and now on up my legs to my thighs and to my hips, just completely relaxing. And my full attention is on relaxing my body as the relaxing power now moves on up into the fingers of both of my hands . . . relaxing my hands. And my forearms are relaxing . . . and my upper arms are relaxing. My fingers and hands and forearms and upper arms are now completely relaxed. And the relaxing power moves on down into the base of my spine. Relaxing the base of my spine . . . and beginning to move slowly up my spine . . . up my spine . . . up my spine, and into the back of my neck and shoulder muscles. And the back of my neck and shoulder muscles are now becoming loose and limp . . . loose and limp . . . just completely relaxed. And the relaxing power now moves on up the back of my neck and into my scalp . . . relaxing my scalp. And the feeling of relaxation now drains on down into my facial muscles, relaxing them. My jaw is relaxed. I leave a little space between my teeth. And my throat is relaxed. My entire body is now relaxed all over in every way . . . and all tension is gone from my body and mind.

SPIRITUAL PROTECTION

And I now draw a beam of shimmering, iridescent white light down from above. This is the Universal Light of Life Energy . . . the God Light. I imagine it . . . I create it with the unlimited power of my mind. And the light enters my crown chakra of spirituality at the top of my head. I feel it beginning to flow through my body and mind . . . flowing through my body and mind, and beginning to concentrate around my heart area. And I now imagine the light emerging from my heart area and totally surrounding my body with a protective aura of bright white God light. And I am totally protected. Totally protected. Only my own guides and Masters or highly evolved and loving entities who mean me well will be able to influence me in any way.

DEEPENING

(Visualize yourself in a situation in which you are going down, down, down as you count backward from seven to one. This is very important.)

Number seven: deeper, deeper, deeper, down, down, down. Number six: deeper, deeper, deeper, down, down, down. Number five: deeper, deeper, deeper, down, down, down. Number four: deeper, deeper, deeper, down, down, down. Number three: deeper, deeper, deeper, down, down, down. Number two: deeper, deeper, deeper, down, down, down. Number one. And I am now relaxed and at ease and I feel a sense of deepness. I remain consciously aware of my surroundings, but my body is going to sleep . . . to sleep . . . to sleep. Number seven: deeper, deeper, deeper, down, down, down. Number six: deeper, deeper, deeper, down, down, down. Number five: deeper, deeper, deeper, down, down, down. Number four: deeper, deeper, deeper, down, down, down. Number three: deeper, deeper, deeper, down, down, down. Number two: deeper, deeper, deeper, down, down, down. Number one . . . and I am now in a deep, deep altered state of consciousness.

(Insert the main programming content from the appropriate scripts presented in various chapters.)

AWAKENING

In just a moment I am going to awaken to full beta consciousness, feeling as if I've had a nice, refreshing nap. My head will be clear, and I'll think and act with calm self-assurance, feeling glad to be alive, and at peace with myself, the world, and everyone in it. I will awaken remembering absolutely everything that I experienced in this altered state of consciousness. On the count of five, I will open my eyes and be wide awake. Number one, coming on up now and I sense an expanding spiritual light within. Number two, coming on up and at peace with all life. Number three, coming on up and I sense internal balance and harmony. Number four, I now recall the situation and the room. Number five, wide awake, wide awake!

To induce an altered state of consciousness, you can think the induction to yourself, speak it to yourself or record it. It can be a paraphrased version of my script, for there is nothing magical about my words. Every hypnotist and meditation leader uses different words. My company, Valley of the Sun Publishing, markets many tapes using completely different inductions.

The secret to using the induction effectively is to talk monotonously. Speak at a slow pace in an even, uninflected tone of voice—a monotone—as if you were bored to death, and you'll put everyone to sleep, including yourself. Be sure to review Chapter 2 and complete all the exercises to ensure that you'll be open to receiving any impressions that may come to you.

If you experience an altered-state session once a day for three weeks, you WILL attain your natural level. Once you've attained this level, you probably won't go deeper with each session. Continued work with subjective explorations will, however, result in ever-improving receptivity. In other words, the more you do altered-state regression and psychic work, the better you will get at it.

ALTERED-STATE TIPS

BODY POSITION

For your altered-state work, try to pick a time when you will not be interrupted and a place where it is quiet. You may either sit in a chair or lie down. If you are sitting, be sure both feet are flat on the floor and place your hands on your legs. If you are lying down, place your arms at your sides and do not cross your legs; any weight can feel heavier during hypnosis.

The prone position is best unless it causes you to go to sleep. Avoid altered-state work when you're very tired. Each session conditions your subconscious mind and you don't want to condition it to fall asleep when you go into an altered state. If you fall asleep twice while in the prone position, conduct any further sessions in a sitting position for a few days.

Your subconscious mind contains all of the memories of this life and any other life you've ever lived, but it has very little reasoning power; thus it can easily be programmed contrary to your conscious desires, unless you know how to work with it. There is no danger whatsoever in falling asleep while in an altered state; it is only the habit pattern that is to be avoided.

If you wear contact lenses and normally remove them when you go to sleep, take them out before going into an altered state.

THE ENVIRONMENT

Certain conditions are more conducive than others to doing altered-state work. An overly warm room is much better than a cool one. Darkness helps most people to visualize more effectively, so if you don't have a dark room, use one of the sleep masks available for a few dollars in any drugstore. If your environment is noisy, use earplugs. If you're using a tape, use earphones plugged into your tape player. If it is extremely noisy, you may also want to play another tape at the same time to block out the noise. Sound effects tapes of rain or the ocean are good, and New Age music can also be helpful.

Psychic Center

The psychic center acupressure point is located just below the center of your rib cage and above your stomach. Some people like to apply gentle but firm pressure on this point while they are doing their preparatory deep breathing.

Crystal Enhancement

Quartz crystals are energy enhancers, or amplifiers, and they seem to add an element of coherence and order to subjective reception. But in all fairness, not everyone can expect crystals to produce a dramatic difference in how they receive. For me, the difference seems to be a subtle variation in clarity, but I know from considerable experience that I receive better using a crystal while in an altered state, so I always do. If Tara and I are meditating together, we hold hands with the crystal clasped between our cupped hands.

To use a crystal during an individual altered-state session, hold it in your left hand, palm up, and keep your right hand palm down. In metaphysics, this is called an "open circuit."

Quartz crystals are composed of silicon dioxide and are formed beneath the earth's surface under high heat and pressure. They are not cut. They have grown exactly as they appear, with six sides and six facets (angles) leading to the termination point. But according to crystal authority Dr. Randall Baer, "Quartz originates as a thought form in the universal mind on the higher levels of light and is projected down to the earthly substance that quartz is and will become. Crystals serve as a connector to those higher realms of light and are an access tool to other planes of awareness—a 'window of light' to the higher realms."

You'll have to judge the accuracy of Baer's statement for yourself, but there is plenty of scientific information about crystals. Most important, when pressure is applied to a quartz crystal by squeezing it, hitting it, or even subjecting it to sound waves, the crystal discharges piezo-electricity. The pressure is literally converted into electricity. So, even when you are simply talking in the presence of a crystal, there is an energy transformation taking place within the crystal structure. This is an oscillation or vibration that is transformed into subtle sound waves emitted from the quartz.

Since humans are electromagnetic beings, when you talk to the crystal it sends sounds back to you—sounds that are far too subtle to be consciously heard but that feed into your aura. In addition to spoken sound, today's scientists can measure sonic sound waves that emanate from every part of our bodies. So, just having your crystal close to your physical body causes the crystal to produce corresponding electrical discharges. To put this into scientific perspective, think of early crystal radios. With the help of a coil and speaker, a crystal will audibly reproduce the sound waves that exist in the air.

"When you begin to work with a quartz crystal as a . . . meditation or healing tool, the crystal becomes keyed to your own particular, unique energy blueprint," says Dr. Baer. "It actually becomes coded to you as an extension of your energy being, amplifying, focusing, and emitting energy . . . in very powerful ways."

The strongest energy flow is from the termination point of the crystal through the broadest of the six facets leading to the point. If you want to hold your crystal up to your third eye, place this "window of light" against the center of your forehead. If you tape your crystal to your third eye (brow chakra), place the point up. This technique is ideal when used in an altered state to recall past lives, or in other psychic explorations.

By holding your crystal in your left hand, palm up, and squeezing it slightly, more piezo-electrical energy will be emitted; this, in turn, will flow through your physical and mental body, balancing and energizing your chakra centers.

Double-terminated quartz crystals are crystals that have grown to complete termination at both ends. In other words, they have a point at each end, which makes them ideal for balancing, because they can draw in energy as well as send it out from either end. Doubles are very calming crystals, enhancing balance and internal harmony. They are also ideal for balancing and energizing the chakra centers; simply hold the crystal above each center and rotate it to clear the chakra.

Remember, crystals are amplifiers—they amplify both positive and negative energies. If you are experiencing negative or unpleasant energy, it might be a good idea to set the crystal aside for a while.

RETAINING YOUR ALTERED-STATE IMPRESSIONS

Subjective impressions received while in an altered state may seem dreamlike and fade rapidly when you return to full beta consciousness. For this reason, you might want to have a pencil and paper beside you when you awaken so you can quickly write down the highlights of the session. Or, you could speak into a tape recorder so you can keep your eyes closed and verbally commit your experiences to tape while they are still fresh in your mind.

Many people use a second tape recorder (if you're working with a tape), leaving it on while the first tape plays. They then relate their experiences as the impressions come. The results are the same as in a past-life regression or psychic exploratory session that is directed by a hypnotist. Verbalizing your impressions will not bring you out of an altered state; in fact, it's a great way to keep yourself focused on the input, especially if you have a tendency to drift off or fall asleep.

THE TRIPPING PROBLEM

Once you are fully conditioned, you may sometimes go into an altered state and not remember anything upon awakening. If you are working with a tape and open your eyes on the count of five, you are not just falling asleep. You may actually be too good a subject and be "tripping" or drifting in and out. There are several ways to deal with this tendency.

First, try sitting up against a wall or in a chair while in the altered state. You won't be quite as comfortable, but this may help to keep you from tripping.

If you're simply going too deep, don't do any deep breathing before the induction. Once you have become conditioned, you may also want to limit the body relaxation to simply imagining a wave of relaxation moving from your toes to your head. Another technique is to make sure you stay fully conscious during the initial part of the induction. If you're working with a tape, don't close your eyes and start speaking until you get to the countdown from seven to one (see page 233).

Other techniques that may help if you're falling asleep or tripping out: Niacinamide (vitamin B3) opens up all the deep-level blood vessels within about twenty minutes after you take it. College students often use it to stay fully alert during an exam. I always take about 500 milligrams before going out on stage to conduct a seminar.

A couple of 400 IU capsules of vitamin E and two tablespoons of honey is another upper, especially when combined with a few minutes of strenuous exercise. The honey instantly puts sugar in your system while the vitamin E extends the oxygen. It will keep you wide awake and mentally alert for up to four hours. Don't use this if you've been drinking alcohol as it will work in reverse, as a downer.

SPINNING OR SWAYING

A small percentage of people sometimes experience a feeling of spinning or swaying while in an altered state, especially toward the end of the induction. There is nothing to fear; you are probably attempting to leave your body and astrally project. To stop the effect, simply give yourself the strong command, "stabilize!" You are always in control.

HEADACHE

On rare occasions, someone will awaken from an altered state with a headache that feels like a tight band around the forehead. Although somewhat uncomfortable, it is not a matter for concern and will usually disappear within thirty minutes. The ache can be the result of anxiety about the altered-state experience, but many metaphysicians feel it is the result of "third eye" activity and indicates psychic awakening. Regular use of altered-state techniques often results in an expansion of extrasensory perception, even when the subject isn't trying to be psychic.

TOUCHING OTHERS IN AN ALTERED STATE

Touching others while you and the other person(s) are in an altered state can sometimes create a psychic connection. As an example, let's assume you'd like to explore the concept of a prior shared lifetime. Before conducting the session, make the conscious decision with your partner to seek a previous lifetime you may have shared. Communicate this idea clearly to your subconscious minds. Then go into the altered state holding hands. (This will work best if you make a tape of the regression session.) Once the session is over, verbally compare your results. To be more objective, write down your experiences before sharing them with each other.

ESOTERIC CONSIDERATIONS

Some esoterically oriented people feel that they attain superior results with the metaphysical altered-state sessions by following one or more of these occult principles:
• Go into an altered state in a prone position. Align your body in a north/south direction with your head north.
• Remove all metal jewelry.
• Remove all clothing.
• Surround yourself with three lighted white candles.

Chakra Connection

An intense psychic connection can be established between two people by doing a chakra visualization exercise prior to conducting a joint metaphysical exploration. The chakras are the seven centers of the etheric body. Lie down side by side, hold hands (cupping a crystal); and do your deep breathing. Then one of you will direct the connection:

"We are now going to visualize a connection taking place between the crown chakras of spirituality on the top of our heads. Visualize an intense violet light emanating from the top of your head . . . see it in your mind. It is arcing out, up, across, and over to connect with my head. Make it real with the unlimited power of your mind. It's an intense, shimmering, iridescent violet light connecting our crown chakras. *(Pause.)* The connection is now complete, and it is time to visualize the next chakra connection."

Both people participate in the visualization, and the process continues with the next three chakras:

Third eye, brow chakra (in the center of your forehead)—blue-violet in color.

Throat chakra—silver-blue in color.

Heart chakra—golden in color.

With practice, many couples are capable of perceiving identical impressions, emotions, or regression experiences while in an altered state of consciousness.

Programming and Reprogramming in an Altered State of Consciousness Basic Script

(Use the same deep breathing preparation and induction described at the beginning of this chapter.) And I am now relaxed and at ease and centered upon achieving my goals. I am at peace and feel in balance

and in harmony. A quietness of spirit permeates my body and mind, and I am now going to begin to create the reality I desire to live. I begin by relating several very positive suggestions which will be communicated to every level of my body and mind. I am open to these suggestions which I will accept and act on:

Insert eight to fifteen suggestions phrased positively as an already accomplished fact. As an example, my Master of Life Personality Transformation *videotape for Valley of the Sun Publishing (Video Hypnosis VHS105) contains the following suggestions: I now let go of all fears. I give and receive unconditional love. Negativity flows through me without affecting me. I create my own reality. I draw joyous experiences into my life. I feel balanced and harmonious. I am independent and self-responsible. I create the reality I desire to live. "Master of Life" are my key words for conditioned response.*

These suggestions have been communicated to every level of my body and mind . . . and so it is. And it is now time to use positive visualization and perceive myself having already accomplished my goal of _____. I will see myself in a vivid fantasy in which I _____. I'll make the mental movie real. Playing the role, playing the part and experiencing every detail in my mind. And in so doing, communicate my desires to my subconscious mind, which always assists me by generating circumstances to create my programmed reality.

(Two minutes or more of silence to use for visualization.)

I have just seen my own reality and I am open to new suggestions, which I will accept and act on. *(Repeat the eight to fifteen suggestions again.)* And these suggestions have been communicated to every level of my body and mind . . . and so it is.

And it is now time to use a mantra to saturate my

subconscious mind with a message. *(Phrase your goal positively in one sentence as an already accomplished fact. Examples: "I now take complete control of my life and am happy and fulfilled by my independence." "I now master my tennis concentration, timing, strokes, and strategy." "I love myself, my body, and my immune system, which always keeps me healthy." Repeat the sentence over and over as a mantra ten to twenty times or more.)*

And I am now going to give myself some key trigger words for conditioned response. Any time in my daily life that I find myself _____, I will simply stop what I am doing, close my eyes, take a couple of deep breaths, and say these words quietly to myself . . . "_____." The words "_____" are a conditioned-response key to my subconscious mind and when I say these words, I will draw upon the unlimited power of my subconscious mind to support me in the fulfillment of my desires. When I say these key trigger words I will _____. The words "_____" now become my conditioned-response technique and I will experience it as totally effective. And every time I hear this suggestion and every time I use my "_____" programming, it will become more and more effective.

And now, once again, it is time to create another mental movie in which I perceive myself as having already accomplished my _____ goals. *(Pause for two minutes or more for visualization.)*

Awaken

And it is now time to awaken to full beta consciousness, feeling fully rested, calm, and at peace with myself, the world, and everyone in it. I'll be revitalized and filled with energy. On the count of five, I will open my eyes and be wide awake, fully alert, thinking and acting with calm self-assurance. Number one . . . coming on up now. Number two . . . coming on up and feeling a sense of peace and joy. Number three . . . coming on up and I perceive the balance and harmony. Number four . . . I recall the situation and the room. Number five . . . wide awake, wide awake.

An Explanation of the Programming Techniques

MENTAL MOVIES

Mental movies could also be called creative visualizations. They are simply a technique for visualizing your goals as an already accomplished fact. This is probably the most important aspect of altered-state programming.

A mental movie is a fantasy of your own creation. The fantasy is a programming technique for the subconscious mind, which can't tell the difference between imagination and reality. You are the producer, the director, and the actor. You use other people in your movies, but as the director, you control their words, actions, and reactions. You film this movie exactly the way you would like to create your own reality.

The key to successful programming is to make the mental movie as real as possible. See it with your inner eyes. Feel and sense everything that is happening—your emotions and the reactions of others who are observing your victory or accomplishments. Note their facial expressions and other small details. Create the environment just as you would if you were actually producing a movie.

The movie always shows you achieving your objectives . . . viewing them as an already accomplished fact. This is very important—by seeing your goals as already accomplished, your subconscious is able to fully comprehend the goal and immediately begin to work toward making it a reality. Because you are controlling all communications while in the altered state, you maximize your programming power.

MENTAL MOVIE EXAMPLES

Let's say that your goal is to lose weight. Here are three examples of mental movies you might create:

1. You see yourself stepping on the scale after your morning shower. You watch the dial swing, slow down . . . and then stop at your desired weight. You hear yourself exclaim with delight, see the smile on your face, feel the elation as you toss on your robe and run down the hall to tell your husband of your accomplishment. Next, you create his positive reactions, and so on.

2. You are shopping and you run into a friend that you haven't seen for a long time. Your friend is amazed at your thin body and proceeds to tell you so. Create the rest of the dialogue, your reactions, etc.

3. You are in a women's clothing store and the saleslady asks what size dress you wear. You respond with your ideal dress size. Then you try on the dress and realize it's a perfect fit. The saleslady compliments you on your figure.

Try making up many different mental movies; run one today, another tomorrow . . . varying them and producing new ones to fit your situation and goal. Remember, you are limited only by your belief system.

The trigger word technique is post-hypnotic programming to use when you need an extra lift to support your goal. The word you choose might be "concentration," "willpower," "motivation," "energy"—there are any number of possibilities. This standard programming is amazingly effective once you have become conditioned and begun to use it. It's a good idea to wait until you've conducted an altered-state session at least once a day for three weeks before you call on your trigger word programming. Then use it often, because each time you use a conditioned-response trigger word its effectiveness increases.

For example, here is how the trigger-word section of my Master of Life Personality Transformation tape is worded: "And you now become a Master of Life, living in harmony with yourself and your world. And I am now going to give you some key trigger words for post-hypnotic conditioned response. Any time in your daily life that you find yourself needing to recall your dedication to the goal of enlightenment, you will simply stop what you are doing, close your eyes, take a couple of deep breaths and say these words quietly to yourself, 'Master of Life.' The words 'Master of Life' are a conditioned response signal to your subconscious mind and when you say these words, you will experience peace, balance, and harmony. This conditioned-response technique draws upon the power of your subconscious mind to support you in the fulfillment of your enlightenment goal. The words 'Master of Life' now become a post-hypnotic suggestion for mental tranquillity, peace, balance, and harmony. And you will experience the suggestion as totally effective. Every time you hear this suggestion and every time you use your 'Master of Life' programming, it will become more and more effective."

Research Explains Why Altered-State Programming Works

A breakthrough in physics research shows how the use of altered states of consciousness can lead to a transformation in nearly every part of your life.

An experimentally confirmed theory earned Belgian chemist Ilya Prigogine a Nobel prize. Called "the theory of dissipative structures," it solved the mystery regarding why the use of altered states can result in life-changing insights, new behavior patterns, and the relief of lifelong phobias or ailments. Here's how the theory works as applied to real people:

First, remember that human beings are structures. The structure of your body is composed of bones, muscles, and ligaments. Your brain, however, is given structure by the thoughts and memories that dictate your actions. It is the programming of your brain that provides it with structure.

Now, Prigogine's theory states that complex structures (such as the human brain) require an enormous and consistent flow of energy to maintain. In the brain, that energy is measured as brain-wave levels on an EEG machine. The up-and-down pattern of these wave levels reflects a fluctuation in the amount of energy reaching the brain. The larger the fluctuation of brain-wave levels, the larger the fluctuation of energy.

In wide-awake beta consciousness, your brain-wave levels would show up on an EEG as small, rapid, up-and-down lines. There is little fluctuation in the level of energy. However, when you change your state of consciousness through the use of altered-state techniques—hypnosis, meditation, relaxation, etc.— your brain-wave levels shift to alpha and theta. There is a lot of fluctuation in the level of the energy in these altered states.

According to Prigogine's theory, small fluctuations of energy (such as beta rhythms) are suppressed by the brain, so it stays essentially the same. That's why changes suggested to a conscious mind usually have little effect. The message is suppressed by all the existing programming. However, says Prigogine, large fluctuations of energy (such as alpha and theta rhythms) can cause the structure to break apart and reorganize itself into a higher and even more complex form.

That's why suggestions given to an individual exploring in the alpha and theta brain-wave levels are so effective in creating change. The new suggestion, dropped into the uneven alpha rhythms like a pebble into a pond, creates a ripple effect that tears apart old programming and creates new behaviors and viewpoints. Your brain dismantles its old concepts and reorganizes them into new, more complex, and usually more meaningful forms.

When this shift occurs, you may become aware of information about your life and goals that your old mental structures kept hidden from you. You may experience a sudden, powerful insight into an unsolved problem and you may even release yourself from its effects.

There is also an added bonus. Each transformation makes the next one likelier. You see, every time you trigger a collapse of memory or data structures and your brain reorganizes them into more complex forms, it requires more energy to maintain those new structures. And they are even more vulnerable to fluctuations of energy. Basically, the more complex a structure is, the more unstable it is, and the easier it is to trigger the next transformation.

If you carry this concept to its logical conclusion, you'll see that every time you successfully use an altered state of consciousness to achieve new insights, or to program or reprogram yourself, you increase your chances of success the next time you try it. In other words, the more you seek and find your own answers within, the easier it gets. And the more you'll understand how unhappiness and failure are self-inflicted, while happiness and success are self-bestowed.

Suggested Reading

Reality Therapy
by William Glasser, M.D.
Harper & Row

Profound Simplicity
by Will Schutz
Bantam Books

Actualizations
by Stewart Emery
Doubleday Dolphin

Playing Ball on Running Water
and *Even in Summer the Ice Doesn't Melt*
by David K. Reynolds, Ph.D.
Quill—William Morrow

Discourses and Books
by Bhagwan Shree Rajneesh
17 Koregaon Park
Poona 411001 India

Discourses and Books
by J. Krishnamurti
Harper & Row

*The Donning International Encyclopedic
Psychic Dictionary*
by June G. Bletzer
The Donning Company

About the Author

DICK SUTPHEN (pronounced Sut-fen) is an author, past-life therapist and seminar trainer. His best-selling books— *You Were Born Again to Be Together, Past Lives, Future Loves, Unseen Influences,* and *Pre-destined Love*—have become classic metaphysical titles (Pocket Books).

Sutphen is the author of eleven metaphysical books and over 350 self-help tapes, including past-life re-gression programs. He has spent twenty-one years in New Age work and research. Today he conducts his world-famous seminar trainings throughout the coun-try; since 1977, 85,000 people have attended them. Dick also publishes *Master of Life,* a free, quarterly publication that promotes mental, physical and philo-sophical self-sufficiency and keeps readers abreast of his latest research and findings.

Dick and his wife, Tara, live in Malibu, California, where he writes and directs his New Age communica-tions network. To receive a copy of *Master of Life* magazine, please write: Dick Sutphen, Box 38, Malibu, CA 90265.

Dr. David Viscott,

renowned psychiatrist, reaches out to you with understanding and advice. From self-analysis to exploring your feelings to learning to live with someone else, David Viscott cuts through psycho-babble to help you know and love yourself and the world around you.

BOOKS THAT HELP TO SOLVE YOUR PROBLEMS

____63325 **ART OF SELFISHNESS** David Seabury $4.50

____67325 **BODY LANGUAGE** Julius Fast $4.95

____63006 **LOST IN THE COSMOS** Walker Percy $4.95

____63882 **LUSCHER COLOR TEST** Dr. Max Luscher $4.50

____60385 **MEANING OF ANXIETY** Dr. Rollo May $5.95

____52463 **OG MANDINO'S TREASURY OF SUCCESS UNLIMITED**
ed. Og Mandino $3.95

____67432 **SEEDS OF GREATNESS** Dr. Denis Waitely $4.95

____68405 **STAND UP! SPEAK OUT! TALK BACK!**
The Key to Self Assertive Therapy
Robert E. Alberti & Michael Emmons $4.50

____67137 **SUCCESS THROUGH A POSITIVE MENTAL ATTITUDE**
Napoleon Hill & W.C. Stone $4.95

____63932 **THE SKY'S THE LIMIT** Dr. Wayne Dyer $4.95

____52462 **THE SUCCESS SYSTEM THAT NEVER FAILS**
W. Clement Stone $4.50

____65865 **UP FROM DEPRESSION** Leonard Cammer, M.D. $4.50

____60405 **TOO YOUNG TO DIE** Francine Klagsburn $3.50

____63204 **YOU CAN STOP SMOKING**
Jacquelyn Rogers $3.95

____66749 **BEING THE BEST** Denis Waitley $4.50

____67003 **THE SELF TALK SOLUTION**
Shad Helmstetter $4.50

____63587 **EVERYTHING TO LIVE FOR**
Susan White–Bowden $3.95

____66647 **WHAT TO SAY WHEN YOU TALK**
TO YOURSELF Shad Helmstetter, Ph.D $4.50

____66125 **STAYING SOBER** Judy Myers $7.95

**POCKET
BOOKS**